A Beautiful Mind

A Biography on Dr. Austin Mardon

Dr. Austin Mardon

Alyssa Wu

Wan Ling Dai

Sameen Ali

Irene Falade

Sathurthika Selvanayagam

Michael Phan

Isra Ziad

David Henneberg

Tara Chen

Suhaib Aldada

Noah Varghese

A Beautiful Mind

A Biography on Dr. Austin Mardon

Typeset and Cover Design by Keighly Gibson

ISBN: 978-1-77369-898-4

Ebook ISBN: 978-1-77889-017-8

Golden Meteorite Press

103 11919 82 St NW

Edmonton, AB T5B 2W3

www.goldenmeteoritepress.com

GM★
P R E S S

Table of Contents

Section 3:

COVID-19 Impact

Section 4:

Conversational Topics

Section One:

A Biographical Synopsis of Dr. Austin Mardon

Chapter 1:

A history of schizophrenia in the Mardon family

Written by: Sameen Ali

Introduction

The exact causes of symptoms for schizophrenia is still unknown. However, research has shown multiple factors such as physical, genetic, psychological and environmental factors that can make a person more likely to develop the illness (NHS, 2019). Having a stressful and emotional life can trigger psychotic episodes. Mostly, schizophrenia tends to run in families; however, there is no single gene that is found to be responsible (NHS, 2019).

Dr. Mardon has a family history of schizophrenia. Not only was he diagnosed with schizophrenia; however, the same symptoms persisted in his mother, first cousin, and great grandmother. Different combinations of genes are likely to make certain individuals more vulnerable to develop the condition.

Inheritance of schizophrenia is studied from twins. For identical twins, it was found that if one twin develops schizophrenia, the other twin has a 50% chance of developing it too. This is true even if they are raised separately (genetic factors). For non-identical twins who have different genetic makeup, when one twin develops schizophrenia, the other has a 12.5% of developing schizophrenia. These findings suggest that genes are the only factor influencing schizophrenia. This chapter discusses Austin Mardon's story of diagnosis with schizophrenia; in addition, it discusses his experience with the illness.

What is schizophrenia?

Schizophrenia is a serious mental illness. The impact it has on a person goes beyond physical, it includes how the person feels and thinks (NIMH, 2022). Someone who has schizophrenia will lose touch with reality (NIMH, 2022). Not only is this distressing for the individual experiencing these symptoms, but also for family and friends. The symptoms impact day-to-day activities which a person participates in. Symptoms of schizophrenia are seen at early ages, the diagnosis is most common for ages 16-30; this is also when the individual experiences psychosis (NIMH, 2022). Research has depicted that symptoms are usually present before the first episode of psychosis; however, treatment occurs much later. Schizophrenia is also much more rare for younger children. Symptoms for individuals experiencing looks very different from person to person (NIMH, 2022). However, there are commonalities between all schizophrenia patients these include psychotic symptoms, negative symptoms and lastly, cognitive symptoms.

Psychotic symptoms mostly change the way the individual thinks, acts and perceives the world (NIMH, 2022). These symptoms result in loss of reality and experiencing others and the world in a distorted way. For many patients, these symptoms come and go. This was the case for Dr. Mardon as well. A list of psychotic symptoms include (NIMH, 2022):

- **Hallucinations:** When an individual hears, smells, tastes or feels things that are not actually there. For many people with this illness, they hear sounds or voices from people. This may include family and friends (Mayoclinic, 2020).
- **Delusions:** When an individual has strong beliefs that are false. It may seem irrational to others; however, it is the truth for that individual (Mayoclinic, 2020). They may think someone is about to hurt them, when they are not etc.
- **Movement disorder:** when a person experiences abnormal movement; for example, they may keep repeating a specific movement over and over again (Mayoclinic, 2020).
- **Thought disorder:** a thought disorder refers to individuals who have a way of thinking that is illogical. They find it difficult to speak or have trouble organising their thoughts. They may stop in the middle of a thought or jump from different topics (Mayoclinic, 2020).

Negative symptoms include loss of motivation and interests which leads to lack of enjoyment in daily activities and withdrawal from social life (Mayoclinic, 2020). This also leads to a difficulty in showing emotions and being able to function normally. Negative symptoms include: being unable to plan activities and execute them, such as grocery shopping. Having trouble feeling enjoyment or pleasure in daily life (Mayoclinic, 2020). Talking in a dull voice that shows lack of interest or very limited facial expressions. The individual suffering starts to sound like a robot (NIMH, 2022). They begin to avoid social interactions and have very low energy throughout the day. In extreme cases, an individual may stop moving or talking which is a rare condition known as catatonia (NIMH, 2022).

Lastly, individuals may also experience cognitive symptoms. These include problems in concentration, attention and memory (NIMH, 2022). These symptoms make it very difficult for the individual to hold onto a conversation, learn new things or remember activities such as appointments. Having cognitive abilities impact daily life which makes it difficult to process new information, make decisions and use information that was learned (Mayoclinic, 2020). In addition, it becomes very difficult to focus or pay attention to certain things.

Most individuals with schizophrenia are not violent; however, people with schizophrenia are more likely than those without the illness to be harmed. For people with schizophrenia the risk of self harm is more significant than other illnesses, this also includes violence to others (Mayoclinic, 2020). Hence, it is best to get treated as soon as possible.

Schizophrenia tends to run in families (NIMH, 2022). Research also shows that brain structure and function shows that people with schizophrenia may have different brain sizes in certain areas compared to others (NIMH, 2022). These differences can begin to develop at birth. Research is working towards understanding how brain structure and function are related to schizophrenia (NIMH, 2022).

Before Mardon was Diagnosed

Austin displayed symptoms of schizophrenia from an early age. His father had warned him that this was something that ran in the family. And the symptoms were explicit. However, as life progressed, he realised that his personality traits were symptoms of the illness. For example, in social situations Austin would get nervous, he was known as the freak who would speak to himself. Austin's father noticed unusual behaviours in him as well. For example, Austin's tendency to hear voices and his speaking to himself. However, in earlier life Austin was able to ignore these symptoms and lead a fairly normal life. However, it was much more difficult for them compared to any other person. He planned on getting a PhD in geography and to achieve his goals he enrolled in University of Lethbridge in Alberta, Canada. One of Austin's professors invited him to accompany a group of scientists leading NASA/NAF to Antarctica. Austin was thrilled to take this opportunity (Mardon, 2010).

It is said that schizophrenia can be caused due to a traumatic event that triggers it. For Austin, the traumatic event led to increased symptoms to the point where they were no longer able to ignore them. He could not continue his day to day life. This began when he prepared for his Antarctic expedition. In October 1986, at 24 years old, Austin finally arrived at Antarctica where there were bodies of workers who had died in a hiking accident. The bodies were lying in a field. Austin faced many near death experiences himself. From his journey he developed post traumatic stress disorder, nerve damage, frozen lungs, frost bits and altitude sickness. After returning from his trip, Austin attempted to live his normal life; however, now his schizophrenia was worse than ever.

Due to his trip, in 1990 Russian sport organisations began to contact Austin Mardon. They informed him that he was going to go on a journey to the Soviet high arctic and another Antarctic journey. When he arrived in Russia, he was interrogated. There was no expedition. However, they would not let him leave. Through the help of the Canadian embassy, he was able to return home (Mardon, 2010).

These occurrences all served to increase his schizophrenia. Upon returning from Russia, Austin was unable to go back to "normal" no matter how much he tried. Around this time he began to experience positive symptoms such as hallucinations. In October 1992, Austin's hallucinations eventually lead to a psychotic break. Due to his schizophrenia, Austin believed that there was a grand conspiracy. He always heard people whispering, and he didn't like individuals who wore black. In addition, he was unable to sleep and had many, racing thoughts which resulted in restlessness.

With all that was going on, Austin still did not believe his symptoms were due to schizophrenia. He was in denial. However, Austin was suffering. He was unable to turn off his brain. The hallucinations began to appear more powerful. The particular incident that resulted in Austin finally being admitted to the hospital was a hallucination regarding religion. The hallucination led him to St Agnes church where he began to crawl up the stairs (Mardon, 2010). However, an usher found him and took him to the hospital. The hospital took him and his illness became clear. He was no longer able to ignore it.

Thinking back to his life, the earliest symptom in his family was on Austin's maternal side. It occurred right after the birth of his grandfather in 1890. Austin's mother was diagnosed with schizophrenia when he was 5. As a result, his father developed a heart condition. He was under a tremendous amount of stress. During the time period his mother developed schizophrenia, there was no medication to help her. She didn't recognize the illness and instead resorted to locking herself up in a room. His mother expressed anger at her illness. At what it took away from her, the possibility of a healthy life. However, upon reflecting Austin does not feel the same anger. Instead he felt disappointed. He could have accomplished much more if it wasn't for the illness. Austin Mardon discusses that there has always been a lot of shame regarding the topic.

Getting Diagnosed

Austin Mardon grew up with schizophrenia, it was quite obviously apparent in his family. Although he grew up with it present in his life, he still found it a challenge to pinpoint that the symptoms he was experiencing was due to schizophrenia. He felt he was becoming robotic, just trying to complete day-to-day tasks and even struggling to do those. When the incident happened in St Agnes church, he was taken to the hospital where he was finally diagnosed. From here, his treatment began. Schizophrenia occurs because of an imbalance of chemicals in the brain. Since the factors of this disease are not completely known, it can be a variety of things. As for Austin Mardon's case, it was the life leading up to his traumatic, exhausting and stressful experiences that triggered his symptoms to become more severe. In addition, it also ran in the family. This means there was a genetic tie. Although there is no gene that scientists have associated with schizophrenia, from twin studies it is clear that there is a direct link. For Austin, the disease ran in the maternal side of his family. This had a big impact.

Upon being diagnosed with this illness, Austin heard the bad news "there is no cure for schizophrenia". In the back of his mind, Austin was already aware of this factor from having seen his family members struggling. The news was nonetheless, still devastating. Although there is no treatment there are medications that doctors can prescribe to help suppress the symptoms that schizophrenia gives. Although these medications have many, many side effects, they reduce the life-threatening symptoms to help the patient continue his day to day life. Through technology and countless experiments, research today has become more advanced when it comes to medication. These new medications are known to be safer and more effective, a luxury that Austin's mother, grandmother, and cousin did not have.

Medications that target symptoms include both positive and negative symptoms of schizophrenia. When Austyin was diagnosed, the treatment options were not a concern to him. This is due to how bad his schizophrenia had developed. He did not care about the options available. Instead, Austin was hopeless and just wanted to isolate from society. He began to think how different his life would be if this "curse" had not plagued his life and his family's life. Not only is schizophrenia genetic, it also impacts individuals you are living with. For example, as mentioned before, Austin's father was incredibly impacted by his mother's diagnosis to the point where he developed heart complications. Austin began asking himself life questions: if I did not have this disease, what would I do with my life, what about my career and how would his life be different?

These thoughts, and feelings lead to Austin denying the medications he was given in the hospital. He did not want to ingest anything. Unfortunately, this is a common act done by schizophrenic patients. Refusing to take medications has escalated many patients' lives for the worst. This is common for schizophrenics because to the patient, it feels as if the medical staff are attempting to kill them. This was the same situation for Mardon. He became stubborn to the point where the staff at the hospital called in Austin's father to speak to him in order to get the required medication. Him and his father had a long conversation to which Austin would be persuaded to fight this illness with all that he had.

Entering Society with a Diagnosis

When Asutin left the hospital, he felt alone. Misunderstood. He felt like an outlier. No one understood his situation. As a result, Austin isolated himself from the world. Not only did he feel left out and misunderstood but he felt embarrassed. He did not talk to his friends and family, instead there would always be silence. He drifted apart from people he was most close to. Austin also broke up with his girlfriend at that time. In addition, Austin felt as if the individuals around him looked at him differently. Now that he had a diagnosis, he felt as if people treated him differently too. This was very difficult for him and took a mental toll. As a result, life became meaningless and hollow.

Life with Illness

Now, Austin was living life while taking multiple medications. These are known as antipsychotic medications. There are two categories of antipsychotics, this includes atypical (newer forms of the medication) and typical (traditional forms of medication). Typical medication blocks dopamine receptors to counter the higher levels of neurotransmitters in schizophrenia patients (Li, 2016). One of the factors that motivated Austin to continue his life as normal was a reminder of the conversation he had with his father. In addition, Austin knew he was not the only one suffering. He wanted to help others and drive impact. Although his schizophrenia was difficult, he was reminded of the challenges his mother had to overcome. Keeping all these factors in mind, Austin was able to accept his illness. He saw his limitations but he also saw what he was capable of. In a way, this set him free. Since his diagnosis, he had given up on multiple aspects of his life. For example, driving, paying back student loans, not completing his PhD and he had accepted the fact that he would never have a full time job. However, he wanted to make the most of his situation. As a result, he began volunteering for Alberta's schizophrenia society, and club house society in Edmonton. Although becoming an active member was difficult and a slow process, the important part was that Austin had begun to put his hardwork and effort in.

Austin recognized that having a goal in life to keep him moving forward was essential, to him this goal was helping clothes through his volunteer work with the schizophrenia society. Through that he was shocked to learn how many patients refused to take their medication. This had severe impacts on them. Austin never missed his medications. This resulted in him developing many secondary issues such as weight gain (450lbs), diabetes, and blood pressure. However, the symptoms were alleviated. Although Austin could not live a luxurious life, he was satisfied with what he had. He also knew that he would have to retire early due to his condition. From taking his illness seriously and continuing his medication, this allowed Austin to live an influential and successful life despite his limitations and concerns. Austin began volunteering at a schizophrenia self support group known as "Unsung Heroes" he eventually became the co-chairman.

In November 1997 Austin was awarded for all his volunteer work. Despite his illness he had progressed tremendously. He had come to terms with his illness and decided to take action. Life had its ups and downs but through religion and his belief in God as a catholic, it kept him firm. His religion also added meaning to his life and helped him cope. Before his diagnosis and hard work, Austin expressed how he was on a government pension which saved his life, otherwise would have been homeless. Having that safety net is essential, all individuals who suffer from illness require it.

Receiving awards such as Governor General's Caring Canadian Award was a life changing, powerful and empowering moment for Austin Mardon. This success gave Austin the confidence required to become comfortable in himself and his ability. In 2005, his friend encouraged him to go on a catholic dating website to search for a life partner. Austin finally mustered the courage to create a profile. After creating a profile, a woman named Catherine contacted him. Catherine would become his wife. At first he was afraid to share his illness with her, but she has had a lot of prior experience with mental illness. Austin was blessed and incredibly happy that he had found a woman who has intense love for him.

Conclusion

With Catherine in his life, Austin felt complete. After his marriage with her, he had a lot of success in his life. Austin had never in a million years thought that he would be as successful as he is. He didn't think he would accomplish so much. Although he was grateful for his opportunities and awards, his family thought Austin received them out of sympathy. This was not the case and Catherine was proud of him nonetheless. When reflecting on his journey, Austin recognizes that it is not necessarily the illness itself that hindered him, but rather his reaction. His withdrawal from society and embarrassment. Soon as he overcame those aspects, there was much blessing and reward in his life. Austin Mardon now makes it a mission to help other individuals who are suffering from Schizophrenia. He wants to help them through his first hand experiences.

References

Li, P., Snyder, G. L., & Vanover, K. E. (2016). Dopamine Targeting Drugs for the Treatment of Schizophrenia: Past, Present and Future. Current topics in medicinal chemistry, 16(29), 3385–3403. https://doi.org/10.2174/1568026616666 160608084834

Mardon, Austin, et al. Thriving With Schizophrenia. 2010.

Mayoclinic. "Schizophrenia." Mayo Clinic, Mayo Foundation for Medical Education and Research, 7 Jan. 2020, https://www.mayoclinic.org/diseases-conditions/schizophrenia/symptoms-causes/syc-20354443.

NIMH. "Schizophrenia." National Institute of Mental Health, U.S. Department of Health and Human Services, May 2022, https://www.nimh.nih.gov/health/topics/schizophrenia.

NHS. "Causes - Schizophrenia." NHS, 11 Nov. 2019, https://www.nhs.uk/mental-health/conditions/schizophrenia/causes/.

Chapter 2:

The story of the Antarctica expedition & Receiving the Order of Canada

Written by: Irene Falade

Antarctic Expedition

What exactly is an Antarctic expedition? The Antarctic expedition is a search organised by the National Science Foundation and NASA to look for meteorites that had fallen into the ice-filled mountains. This expedition has been going on for decades and continues to still be active in the ongoing search to recover the extraterrestrial rocks in Transantarctic mountains. The Antarctic area is an increasingly popular collection point due to the knowledge and discoveries finding that around two-thirds of the meteorites that have fallen onto earth landed in the Transantarctic mountains (Choi, 2022).

One of the major reasons Choi (2022) lists as to why meteorites are collected from the Antarctic, is due to the fact that the cold and dry nature of the climate on the continent aids in preservation of the outer space rocks. In addition to that, the dark colour of the meteorites also stands out against the stark white environment of the Antarctic making the job of locating them for collection, less taxing on the expeditioners. However, after the landing of the meteorites, the snow began to accumulate over time and then turn into ice which then submerges the extraterrestrial rocks within ice sheets (Choi, 2022).

Choi (2022) states that, these meteorite ice sheets later flow down to the edges of the continent, and while some of them end up in the ocean, the rest become concentrated on the top of the ice sheets. These areas of concentration are referred to as 'blue ice' because of the azure hue the bare ice takes on because of wind and other natural factors (Choi, 2022). According to Choi (2022), a majority of meteorites that have been found over the years were discovered through blue ice. The way this happens is that when Antarctic ice flows in a certain pattern, along with the climate, terrain and other features being in just the right conditions, the space rocks become revealed on the surface of the blue ice (Choi, 2022). This has resulted in easier recovery of the extraterrestrial rocks for researchers on field missions (Choi, 2022).

Dr. Mardon's Experience

Austin Mardon's expedition to the Antarctic was one of such recovery missions. At the young age of 24, Dr. Mardon was recruited by America through NASA and the National Science Foundation to become a part of the 1986-1987 meteorite recovery mission. The team was made up of researchers and various others that had been recruited from all around the world, making an international team of expeditioners. The expedition took place in the southpole, an 11 kilometres journey to recover the meteorites. In its entirety, the entire expedition took around 3 months to be completed, Dr. Mardon and the rest of his research team residing in the southern side of the transantarctic mountains.

The success of this mission is represented by the recovery of 700 meteorites that Dr. Mardon and his team collected. These meteorites were later stored in a nuclear bomb proof shelter that was located in Houston, Texas. This was to preserve their valuable presence in the field of science. Past research on the extraterrestrial rocks have led to the discovery of evidence that there is life on mars, information on the genesis of the solar system and much more. And while Dr. Mardon states that there was no other discovery, outside the space rocks, found on their expedition, the benefits of being a member of the mission were rewarding enough.

When asked, Dr. Mardon expresses that the most important part of the experience for him was the opportunity to contribute to the advancement of science. And in accordance with this, Dr. Mardon reveals that till today, he remains the only Canadian to have found and recovered a lunar meteorite. Which are a special classification of the extraterrestrial rocks. Lunar meteorites also known as 'Lunaites' are meteorites that originated specifically from the moon. While other meteorites come from various other parts of the solar system.

When asked about his inspiration in joining the expedition, Dr. Mardon expressed his dreams from a younger age of wanting to be an explorer. Dr. Mardon took on the Antarctic expedition opportunity because he believed it would jumpstart his career in exploration. However, as it turned out the expedition was the only chance he would get to live out his dreams. Dr. Mardon came back from the Antarctic expedition physically and mentally sick, an occurrence that would follow him from his early 20s till now.

Mental Illness among Explorers

Mental illness among Antarctic explorers is unfortunately not new, it is actually a very common occurrence. According to an article written by Claire Armitstead in 2018, mental illness has been plaguing explorers for years but it is only recently that it is properly understood. Armiststead (2018), quotes a one explorer, Raymond Priestley, who believed that Antarctic exploration would be a field worth investigating for psychological research. The reason Priestley gives being that, "peculiar madness [had] played a major or a minor part in most expeditions" (Armitstead, 2018). Armitstead (2018) claims that Priestley's suggestion was what led to the beginning of research in 1984, that brought about the identification of Seasonal Affective Disorder also known as SAD. This is a depressive disorder that occurs mainly between the months of September to April.

Apart from that, more awareness on the depression suffered by polar explorers was by a historian named Haddelsey, during his research into the lives of heroic explorers (Armitstead, 2018).

One such hero was JR Stenhouse, a member of the Shackleton's Endurance mission and also a decorated hero from the first World War (Armitstead, 2018). Due to his participation in the first world war, Armitstead (2018) writes that Stenhouse developed a severe case of Post-Traumatic Stress Disorder also known as PTSD. This knowledge was found in Stenhouse's 15 years old diary that detailed his symptoms and struggles (Armitstead, 2018).

Through this Haddelsey is able to discover that the mental illness faced by explorers in the Antarctic can be split into two major categories (Armitsstead, 2018). Armitstead (2018) reports that the first category consists of physiological causes, while the second category consists of psychological or psycho-social factors. With the physiological factor, the depressive disorder of Seasonal Affective Disorder falls into the category. This is because Seasonal Affective Disorder has to do with an increased production of melatonin by the body's pineal gland during extended periods of darkness and no light (Armitstead, 2018). This condition is unpredictable when it comes to determining which individuals might be affected and to what level it affects them as well because in some cases, a sun lamp can ease symptoms according to Armitstead (2018).

While the psychological or psycho-social causes are more often than not linked to pre-existing conditions. They can escalate in a disruptive manner that is dangerous to the individual suffering from it, if they are put in a confined community (Armitstead, 2018). One such example of this is Stenhouse with his PTSD. While it is not clear which category Dr. Mardon might fall under, it is clear that his experience on the expedition did result in harsh mental effects.

Reading through this one might wonder if there was anything that could have been done to avoid the development of the sicknesses. Dr. Mardon responds to this by stating that the Antarctic expedition was similar to going off to a war, there was always going to be casualties, it was unavoidable and he just happened to be one of them. The conditions on the meteorite recovery mission were very harsh, it was high altitude, very cold, isolated. The strength exerted during the expedition in such a terrible and difficult environment were what caused the physical and mental illness Dr. Mardon gained. The mission was physically and mentally demanding.

Dr. Mardon added that the motto of the American Airforce Academy represented the determination he had, "Integrity First. Service Before Self. Excellence in All We Do." He believes that exploration is about sacrifice and pushing boundaries, all of which he did during his journey. He even received an award from the United States government, a medal for his service in the Antarctic expedition. This medal was called the U.S. Antarctic Service Medal. The U.S. Antarctic Service Medal was offered in honour to civilians that had participated in an Antarctic expedition (United States Antarctic Program, n.d.). They had to have been deployed to an Antarctic research station or a vessel and not only that, but they had to stay south of 60 degrees South latitude according to the United States Antarctic Program (n.d.) This was the only way they could be eligible for receiving the Antarctica Service Medal and a Certificate from the National Science Foundation (United States Antarctic Program, n.d.).

As Dr. Mardon was a civilian from Canada that was offered this opportunity and spent the entirety of his mission in the south pole for 3 months collecting meteorites in service to America, it is clear how he rightfully earned the award. Dr. Mardon's experience and journey into the Antarctic for the meteorite collection expedition is a story of courage, determination, and dedication to the field of science. It is a story that should serve as inspiration to other young researchers or individuals interested in the sciences and exploration in the Antarctic. Take the opportunity as it comes to you and let your mind be in service to the growth of knowledge in extraterrestrial discoveries.

Order of Canada

Another notable achievement of Dr. Austin Mardon is the honor he was given in being nominated and awarded the Order of Canada. The Order of Canada was created with the idea of it being a way for Canada to honor its citizens that have made extraordinary contributions to the country (The Governor General of Canada, n.d.). It was created in 1967 by Queen Elizabeth II and referred to as, "cornerstone of the Canadian Honours System" (Canada. ca, 2022). The award was applicable to any and everyone in all sectors of Canadian society that were recognized for their amazing achievements, dedication to the community and service to the Canadian nation (Canada.ca, 2022). According to Canada. ca (2022), there is no specific criteria for what contributions a nominee was required to make, only that it bettered the lives of others and made a difference to the country of Canada.

There are three levels to this award for the awardees, Companion (C.C.), Officer (O.C), and Member (C.M). The first one, Companion (C.C.), is the highest possible level of achievement that is awarded to those individuals recognized for national pre-eminence, their international service or achievements (McMaster University, n.d., The Governor General of Canada, n.d.). And it is not just their work for Canada but also their work for the entirety of humanity (The Governor General of Canada, n.d.). The second, Officer (C.O.), is a step down from the Companion level, but still remains a high degree of merit to individuals that are recognized for their contributions to Canada and humanity, which is not all that different from Companion (The Governor General of Canada, n.d.). Finally, the third and final level, Member (C.M.), is regarded for individuals with contributions focused on a specific community, group or activity (The Governor General of Canada, n.d.). According to the Governor General of Canada (n.d.), it is possible for those who held their levels of Officer and Member to rise in position and have their further achievements acknowledged by the Order of Canada, resulting in a promotion. The general timeline for such promotion is stated to be five years after the initial awarding of the Order of Canada (The Governor General of Canada, n.d.). The Order of Canada is overseen and administered by the Chancellery of Honours at Rideau Hall (Canada.ca, 2022).

This understanding of the Order of Canada is backed by Dr. Mardon's explanation of the award. When asked he describes it as a lifetime charity that is awarded by the Governor General, individuals with a substantial achievement to Canada are nominated for it. As to the information on who nominates these individuals, Dr. Mardon states that he is unaware and was never told who put his name up for nomination of the Order of Canada.

Nominations and Eligibility for Award

According to the Governor General of Canada website, nominations can be made by anyone and everyone. There is no deadline set for when nominations can be made. Nominators are required to prepare examples of the contributions and qualities of their chosen candidates that meet the eligibility criteria of the Order of Canada to explain why they deserved to be nominated (The Governor General of Canada, n.d.). Along with this, the candidates contact information is provided, as well as names and contact information of three references that could support the nomination and validate the candidate's accomplishments (The Governor General of Canada, n.d.). The Governor General of Canada (n.d.) website confirms Dr. Mardon's earlier claim that candidates are unaware of who nominates them because it states that candidates should not be made aware of their nomination in the situation where it does not succeed. It also mentions that The Chancellery of Honours maintains the confidentiality of all nominations and only provides information on an individual's entry to the person that nominated them for the Order of Canada (The Governor General of Canada, n.d.).

As for the eligibility criteria for the Order of Canada, there are a few requirements that are set for a person to fit before they should be even considered as a nominee. The Governor General of

Canada website writes that nominees can be any currently living Canadian citizen, however elected judges and officials cannot receive nominations until they are out of office. Nominations for groups and couples are also not accepted, only individuals can be nominated and group members must have separate nominations (The Governor General of Canada, n.d.). In addition to this, the relations between the group members' contributions has to be explained in the application (The Governor General of Canada, n.d.). Following this, the Governor General of Canada website mentions that living non-Canadians can actually be nominated for the Order of Canada, but their achievements have to be related to or have benefited the people of Canada or the nation itself. Nominations are also made for the promotions of people who are already members of the Order to be moved up to a higher ranking such as Officer, or Companion as explained previously (The Governor General of Canada, n.d.). Previous candidates that had been nominated for the award, but were not selected/approved for the Order of Canada are allowed to be nominated again around five years after the last application (The Governor General of Canada, n.d.). The final rule of eligibility is that posthumous meaning after death nominations of individuals are not allowed or considered (The Governor General of Canada, n.d.).

This entire process of appointing people into the Order of Canada and awarding them the membership is said to sometimes take up to to years of research and review (The Governor General of Canada, n.d.). This review and research of candidate applications is done by an advisory council who then provide the Governor General with their recommendations based on their findings, it is entirely non-partisan and merit-based (The Governor General of Canada, n.d.).

Honor of the Order of Canada

The Order of Canada is a big award and one of the worries Dr. Mardon had, was the fear of not being able to handle the stress that comes with it. Getting appointment into the Order of Canada would make him a public figure as it did other recipients of the award before himself, which was an important duty. Dr. Mardon stated that he was one of the more extensively researched candidates as well.

Regardless of the responsibility however, when asked about how he felt about receiving the Order of Canada, Dr. Mardon replied that it was a truly great honor for himself. He also stated that the Order of Canada to him represented the greatest accomplishment/achievement of his entire life. Although it was also a huge responsibility, because to Dr. Mardon this award was like the country of Canada saying that they wanted to celebrate you, that is the candidate, and make you into a role model for history. This is not a role that can be held lightly and is rather very important and meaningful. Dr. Mardon regarded however that some celebrities that received the Order of Canada did not take it so seriously. For example, Wayne Gretzky, the famous former Canadian ice hockey player and head coach. Apparently, even though he received a nomination and was selected to join the ranks of the Order of Canada, Wayne Gretzky failed to attend his award ceremony for several years. Which shows differing belief systems between two

Order of Canada members, one that held the honor at the highest regard, and one that did not.

Dr. Mardon mentions an interesting fact about how the Order of Canada is regarded highly and looked at by other nations because it is an appointment not based on or related to political affiliations or decisions. This is dissimilar to many other countries and their award honours.

The Antarctica expedition Dr. Mardon embarked on in his earlier years was detailed previously in this chapter so it is safe for one to assume that there is a connection between that and the Order of Canada. However, this is denied by Dr. Mardon, he says his work on the Antarctica expedition for meteors was not tied to his nomination or acceptance into the Order of Canada. The reason behind his membership however, was that Dr. Mardon had frequently told his personal story with mental illness, after he was diagnosed with schizophrenia in 1992. Dr. Mardon was rightfully recognized for becoming a spokesperson and inspiration to thousands of Canadians that are also struggling with their mental health and illness. This is what made him an ideal Order of Canada candidate and also gifted him his award in 2006.

References

About. AICOfficial. (n.d.). Retrieved December 4, 2022, from https://www.antarcticinstituteofcanada.ca/about-3

Armitstead, C. (2018). How the 'blues' of polar heroes throws light on sad syndrome. The Guardian. Retrieved December 4, 2022, from https://www.theguardian.com/society/2018/oct/13/polar-explorers-sad-syndrome-sufferers-new-book

Choi, C. Q. (2022). Meteorite hunters rejoice: Antarctica probably harbors 300,000 undiscovered space rocks. Space.com. Retrieved December 4, 2022, from https://www.space.com/antarctica-undiscovered-meteorites-artificial-intelligence-program

Government of Canada. (2022). Canada.ca. Retrieved December 4, 2022, from https://www.canada.ca/en/department-national-defence/services/medals/medals-chart-index/member-order-canada-cm.html

Office of the Secretary to the Governor General. (2021). Eligibility. The Governor General of Canada. Retrieved December 4, 2022, from https://www.gg.ca/en/honours/canadian-honours/order-canada/eligibility

Office of the Secretary to the Governor General. (2022). Nominate someone. The Governor General of Canada. Retrieved December 4, 2022, from https://www.gg.ca/en/honours/canadian-honours/order-canada/nominate-someone

Office of the Secretary to the Governor General. (2022). Order of canada. The Governor General of Canada. Retrieved December 4, 2022, from https://www.gg.ca/en/honours/canadian-honours/order-canada

Office of the Secretary to the Governor General. (2022).

Levels and insignia. The Governor General of Canada. Retrieved December 4, 2022, from https://www.gg.ca/en/levels-and-insignia

Office of the Secretary to the Governor General. (n.d.). Mr. Austin A. Mardon. The Governor General of Canada. Retrieved December 4, 2022, from https://www.gg.ca/en/honours/recipients/146-7799

Office of the Secretary to the Governor General. (n.d.). Mr. Austin A. Mardon. The Governor General of Canada. Retrieved December 4, 2022, from https://www.gg.ca/en/honours/recipients/146-7799

The USAP Portal: Science and support in Antarctica - Antarctica Service Medals and certificates. (n.d.). Retrieved December 4, 2022, from https://www.usap.gov/travelanddeployment/510/

Chapter 3:

Meeting the Pope

Written by: David Henneberg

History of the Pope

The Pope has been a figure of modern civilization for over 2000 years, with the first Pope Simon Peter reigning from 30AD to 64AD. A pope has existed ever since - apart from a pope passing away - in which there have been varied periods of time without a serving pope. The length of time without a serving pope has never spanned longer than 6 months, however. The current pope today is Pope Francis. The longevity of the papacy is most impressive. As Dr. Austin Mardon puts it, "The catholic Church thinks in Millenia."

The Pope is the head of the Catholic Church and the Bishop of Rome. The Pope is also "the head of the sovereign city-state, Vatican City" (Pappas, 2013). According to Pappas, "the pope meets with heads of state and maintains diplomatic relationships with more than 100 nations. He conducts liturgies, appoints new bishops and travels." (Pappas, 2013). This means that the job of the pope is quite comprehensive, in that the papacy deals with a wide variety of key issues today. The position is held in such high esteem that hordes of religious (and non-religious) people attend his sermons. Pappas continues, "the pope also ministers directly to the faithful, greeting pilgrims at General Audiences, which usually attract between several thousand and tens of thousands of people" (Pappas, 2013). Pappas also mentions that "these nonstop duties are relatively new ... before Pope Paul VI, who held office from 1963 to 1978, popes rarely traveled and had fewer political duties" (Pappas, 2013).

It is interesting to note that the history (which again, spans millennia) has changed over time with the most aggressive changes coming into fruition in recent times. The impressive relevancy of the papal position over such a great span of time cannot be understated, with the Pope regularly dealing with political shifts in ideology and religious backlash from the history of the Catholic Church to this day.

The current Pope, Pope Francis, has an agenda that is startling to some in the church, and being warmly embraced by others. "Pope Francis and his push for openness - toward migrants, Muslims and gay people... Francis has by now made his agenda abundantly clear ... Francis wants an inclusive church that welcomes back into the fold Catholics who have felt geographically, pastorally and ideologically alienated." (Horowitz, 2021) The shifts and changes being made by the now 85 year old Pope reflect the change that is going on in society as well as in the Catholic church itself. Dr. Mardon says - regarding this positive change - that "change is slow, but there is always change. It just takes a while when you have something as big as the Catholic church to contend with."

Background of Dr. Austin Mardon

Although one can google Austin and find out the incredible journey his life has been thus far, Hannah Brockhaus from Catholic News Agency has a great summarization of some of his major accomplishments as well as outlining some of the turbulence he has endured:

"A scientist by education, Austin was part of a NASA meteorite recovery expedition to the Antarctic in the 1980s at the age of 24. Unfortunately, the extreme difficulties of the expedition affected him mentally and physically. Despite these challenges, he earned master's degrees in science and education and published more articles and books, before being diagnosed with schizophrenia, which he manages with medication" (Brockhaus, 2019).

Dr. Austin Mardon has led an adventurous life to say the least. He has travelled around the world on expeditions, been kidnapped by the KGB, written and self-published 50 books, received the Order of Canada (which is Canada's highest level of honour), and met the Pope. And this is in no way a comprehensive list of all the experiences and accomplishments he has had in his 60 years on the planet. The most relevant and interesting part of his impressive resume is that he has done a lot of these things while suffering from schizophrenia. Since his diagnosis at the age of 30, Austin has dedicated much of his time helping others with their battles with grave emotional and mental disorders. The award he received in the form of the Papal Order of Saint Sylvester was a gesture recognizing his incredible and profound efforts supporting those that need it the most.

If one gets the chance to converse with Dr Austin Mardon, they will see that he operates on a highly functioning level and takes advantage of all the blessings he has been given in life. He also reflects on the lessons he has learned through his struggles. When speaking about those suffering from schizophrenia, he says "the best thing for someone in this situation is early identification and intervention, Austin said, 'to give them coping mechanisms to manage it, teach them techniques.'" (Brockhaus, 2019).

Austin Mardon Meets the Pope

Dr. Austin Mardon along with his wife Catherine Mardon met the Pope on November 6th, 2019. The reason for this face-to-face encounter was because Dr. Austin Mardon and his wife received the Pontifical Order of Pope Saint Sylvester, one of five possible orders of knighthood that can be received from the Papal brief. "The Mardons met Pope Francis after the general audience Nov. 6. They were inducted, in 2017, into the Pontifical Order of Pope Saint Sylvester, a papal Order of Knighthood, for their work on behalf of the disabled." (Brockhaus 2019) The Order of St Sylvester "is intended to honor Roman Catholic lay people who are actively involved in the life of the church, particularly as it is exemplified in the exercise of their professional duties and master ship of the different arts." (Order of St. Sylvester, n.d.)

It is important to emphasize that Austin's wife Catherine Mardon also received the reward and was presented with it the same day as Austin. This reward was presented to them by Archbishop Richard Smith on December 21st, 2017.

This is not the only time Dr Austin Mardon had an interaction with the head of the papacy. Dr. Austin Mardon had previously met John Paul II in the 1990's which is an interesting and mind-blowing fact. Very few people get to meet two Pope's in a single lifetime.

An interview was conducted with Dr. Mardon to get his point of view on meeting the Pope, the current state of Catholicism and a few other talking points. Dr. Mardon was compelling when he answered questions and he spoke in a philosophical way. He took into consideration many different angles and he pulled from a profound knowledge of myriad topics. He also had an incredible sense of humour... for example, when asked if he wanted a mention of his encounter with Pope John Paul II, he said "mention the Pope scowling at me because I was fat." And then he laughed. His wishes were kept and of course that golden nugget of information was written down.

Again, Dr. Austin Mardon received the Pontifical Order of Pope Saint Sylvester, a papal order of knighthood - which is one of five possible orders of knighthood that can be given by the papacy.

Archbishop Smith spoke over the rare form of recognition given by the Vatican, he "noted that ... 'it's even more fitting because what Austin and Catherine do is borne of their faith ... Pope Francis is really insistent that we be people of service toward those who are otherwise forgotten, not noticed, left on the peripheries, and sometimes that characterizes those who suffer from mental illness." (Turchansky, 2017)

For those wondering how Dr Austin Mardon and his wife Catherine received such a remarkable award, it is because of the selfless acts they have displayed. Mardon said "(we) primarily got it for the young boys that we've helped. Kids that have aged out of care. 20-25 kids have come through in the last 15 years. It started as an accident." From there, Austin continued, "Father Patrick Baska nominated us - it had to go through a Catholic parish priest. I think we got around 37 letters and the word got around that this was being considered... everyone from cabinet ministers to homeless people writing letters - full spectrum - many with schizophrenia. It was sent to Archbishop Smith." This nomination ignited a flame that would reach Pope Francis himself and would eventually lead to Austin and Catherine receiving this prestigious award. It should be noted that the original nomination put forth by Father Baska was for a lower level of recognition than the Mardon's ended up receiving. When Pope Francis received word of the nomination, he personally upgraded it to the Order of St Sylvester.

When asked if there was anything interesting about his experience in meeting Pope Francis, Austin said "I did kiss the Pope's ring...

Pope Francis and he, uh, did get upset at me and stop talking to me." He continued with a terrific sense of humour, adding that "he hates getting his ring kissed. He just hates it. He actually punched a woman … an old Italian grandmother grabbed his hand to kiss it. He actually punched her... so I'm lucky I didn't get punched." He laughed again.

Catholicism Today

When asked about the state of Catholicism today, Austin likes to remind others that "Catholicism is not a national religion or belief… it spans over every ethnicity, every country, every creed. It really is international, not just spotting here and there."

According to the Institute for Advanced Catholic Studies at USC, 17.7% of the human population is Catholic, which equates to 1.36 billion people. The general thought may be that Catholicism is dwindling and, on the way out, so to speak, but the church has actually been growing year over year to this day, with an added 16 million members in the last year. Dr. Austin Mardon would like to remind everyone that "the catholic corpus takes the long view of centuries and millennia… trying to get civilization to survive … and the human race to survive. Not a lot of people have that kind of long-term view anymore. One unique thing about being Catholic is that we have traditions going back thousands of years, like our Jewish brethren, the Muslims, and the Hindus." Dr. Austin Mardon likes to highlight the many similarities between different religions rather than the differences when he speaks about Catholicism. He carries with him an understanding of the basic needs for all human beings and does not like to focus on the differences from person to person as much as the commonalities.

Without being prompted to speak about the elephant in the Catholic church - the cases of abuse and molestation of young children and the abuse of Indigenous peoples for example - Mardon said "we are all human and to be honest we all make mistakes. Hopefully we can learn from them and ameliorate them." When giving an example of one such potential amelioration, he said "one of the things I proposed to Archbishop Smith was, rather than give settlement money to the first nations, was to offer counselling services on an indeterminate basis. I believe that would be more productive."

Mental Health Today

When talking about some of the issues he sees today over mental health issues he said he urges people to "support the doctors. The doctors are not the enemy. They are over-worked, and they are stressed out ... if you can cooperate with the doctors and the families can cooperate. And you can refrain from (becoming) extremist on the internet. Then I think we could be in a better spot." Austin believes deeply that people holding professional health positions should be given respect. He alluded to misinformation on the internet being a major problem for the scepticism surrounding getting help.

According to the Centre for Addiction and Mental Health (CAMH) "around 450 million people currently struggle with mental illness, making it the leading cause of disability worldwide." (CAMH, 2022) The scope of the problem is almost unfathomable and misunderstood by those that do not suffer (around 7 billion people). The body and mind and the relationship between the two is so complex that it is impossible to carry empathy for those that suffer unless you yourself have suffered or continue to suffer. It may also be possible to comprehend if someone very close to you suffers. The disconnect and elusivity surrounding mental health problems does nothing but exacerbate the problem.

There is also an issue in funding to help those with mental illness. In Ontario for example, "mental illness accounts for 10 percent of the burden of disease … it receives just 7 percent of healthcare dollars." (CAMH, 2022) This reflects the general problem across the entire country. There is very clearly a gap in society's ability to comprehend the issue and how to address it. The sheer amount of information as well as misinformation online can make it difficult for people to understand. This creates a barrier in understanding what mental illness is and how to properly access the care if needed. The lack of funding reflects the lack of urgency seen by the general population on addressing mental health issues today.

Dr. Mardon says that "something that is much more difficult to give than physical support is emotional and psychological support." He went on to say that "homeless people will say 'I'm not ill, everybody else is.'" This highlights the disconnect between the homeless and the rest of the population. Mardon has spent much of his time focussing on addressing key issues in mental health and homelessness. He carries with him an understanding that many do not have, as he himself suffers from schizophrenia. Mardon says that "many talk therapies and medical therapies are so effective that you may not get cured but you can lead a sustainable life." Again, he emphasised the importance of current methods of mitigation for dealing with mental illness. While he admits that the current solutions to mental health may not be perfect in getting rid of all mental health problems, he is sure that it is better than doing nothing. Mardon also notes that "we are on the precipice of major advancements in mental health, but we don't have the social fabric required to implement them." So as far as we have come in treating mental health, there are still many hurdles getting in the way of getting people the help they need.

The changes to our current system need not be rushed, according to Mardon. He said "I believe in evolution rather than revolution. You can make so many mistakes if you don't do things slowly and methodically. That's the whole idea, slow change." He pointed out situations like the Bolsheviks in Russia to help illustrate his point. In that scenario there was a lot of rapid change that took place. But the sudden dismantling of the Czar did not provide a solution to Russia's problems in any kind of perpetuity and left the entire country to suffer for almost an entire century.

A Message of Hope

To help illustrate the difficulties of those dealing with severe mental illness, here is a short story of Martin from the article "New Hope for People With Serious Mental Illness".

"When Martin called 911 to report gunshots, he didn't expect to be arrested and charged with a crime. But there were no gunshots. Martin, who is homeless and has schizophrenia, was experiencing auditory hallucinations. The police arrested him for filing a false report and for methamphetamine possession" (Abrams, 2022). While there are many issues to point out in this short story, it clearly paints the picture that people that struggle from grave mental illness are likely to end up on the streets consuming illicit drugs to self-medicate.

What Dr. Mardon is doing is bringing awareness to this pulsing issue in society. By bringing young people into his home, especially young males (which is the main reason he was awarded the prestigious Order of St. Sylvester), he is giving people that have had a rough beginning a chance to start fresh. When speaking about one of the young males he brought into his home he said, "not to go into details, but he suffered the worst levels of abuse imaginable." These are people that need help, not people that need to be prosecuted. While Martin himself ended up getting treatment from a psychologist, it is noted that "lack of sustained professional support and community resources means that many relapse soon after leaving the hospital" (Abrams, 2022). This problem permeates through most of western civilization. People receive some help while they are at an absolute bottom, and then are unable to access continuous support and revert to their old ways of living. Whether it be homelessness, consuming methamphetamine, or a mix of the two… if a human being is not given consistent treatment over time, they are unlikely to recover.

While this is all sobering to hear, Mardon says that "it is a curse to suffer from mental illness, but it is not the end of the world." He cares deeply that people understand the real difficulties being faced, but he always wishes to send out the simple message of hope. He said "the Catholics have always had hope." When speaking to ways in which we can lead good lives he said, "accept your station in life, which is something the Hindus do." This leads well to the theme of acceptance, which may be the answer to all our problems, Mardon figures. Dr. Andrew Gentile, a psychologist in New York says that "acceptance is a willingness to embrace reality as it is." (Gentile, 2022) He believes that the harsh realities of life can often beat individuals up and have them feeling sorry for themselves - and insists that that is no way to address issues. If individuals focused on the things they can change, rather than the things they are unable to change, they would find themselves in a better mental space. This goes for both those that suffer from mental illness as well as those that do not. There are many ways that mentally healthy people can support those that are suffering, and there are many ways that people with mental illness can help themselves. This is an issue that requires the entire population to work on, together.

References

The Order of St. Sylvester. (2022, November 9). In *Wikipedia*. https://en.wikipedia.org/wiki/Order_of_St._Sylvester

Turchansky, L. (2017). *Advocates for the Mentally Ill Honoured by the Pope.* grandinmedia.ca. https://grandinmedia.ca/advocates-mentally-ill-honoured-pope/

(2022). *The Mental Health Crisis is Real.* camh.ca. https://www.camh.ca/en/driving-change/the-crisis-is-real

Gentile, A., Dr. (2022). *Acceptance is Key!* mindbeacon.com. https://www.mindbeacon.com/strongerminds/acceptance-is-key

Brockhaus, H. (2019, November 19). Catholic couple brings the love of family to young people with mental illness. *Catholic News Agency.*

Pathways Towards Seeking Higher Education

Chapter 4:

Elementary and secondary school education and upbringing

Written by: Isra Ziad

Introduction

From the ages of four to about eighteen, children who later become adolescents spend years of their lives in school. Spending about eight to nine hours at school and it being five days a week, would not really leave much room for surprise if said that school has a significant impact on young minds and molds who they become in the future. The school system encompasses much more than just teaching the basics of math and english, and later to be algebra and literature analyses, yet the environment the student is in, the way the content is taught, and the rate of progression of subjects taught throughout the years, can impact the child's future. Through learning more about Dr. Austin Mardon's upbringing and navigations through the school system, it may shed light on what has been working and what has not when it comes to the next generation of school aged children.

Socialisation aspect of School and its impact on Learning

Dr. Austin Mardon had outlined that school bullying was prevalent during his years in school, specifically in junior high, leaving him feeling isolated and alone. Dr. Mardon was also diagnosed with schizophrenia, and had mentioned that the bullying itself only made his condition worse due to the stress caused through bullying. Unfortunately, it was also noted that even though teachers were sympathetic towards him, that the system as a whole does not protect kids. A 2010 research project that had examined thirty-three Toronto junior high and high schools stated that 49.5% of students surveyed had been bullied online (Canadian Red Cross, n.d.). It can also be hard to report bullying to teachers or to an adult. It was found that over half of bullied children do not report it to a teacher (Canadian Red Cross, n.d.). Important to note that bullying can be done to a child in numerous ways, and is not limited to slurs or bad speech. School children and adolescence can ger physically, sexually, and even virtually bullied (through social media). Bullying and isolation can impact a child's mental health, making them feel less motivated and to thrive less in school and in the world even after their finished school. Given the recent events with the COVID-19 pandemics, many researchers have been adamant on determining the impacts of social isolation on children and adults. With that being said, it has been a major topic of interest to learn more how virtual learning has impacted children. Through socializing, children learn to foster empathy, better their language skills, learn more about the concepts of sharing and collaboration, and gain more confidence (Martin-Pitt: Partnership for Children, n.d.). In a Global News posting, child psychologist, Dr. Mary Avord, had mentioned that she had heard of how children's sadness have turned into depression due to them feeling isolated as a result of the pandemic (Katie Dangerfield, 2020). Isolation from a peer group can have a major impact on a child's social competence and relationship (Katie Dangerfield, 2020). When asked, Dr. Mardon had mentioned that if proper supports were in place, his future could have looked different for him. What can the government do to help children with bullying and socializing in schools? Based on a new release reported in March 2022, the Ontario government is investing over $550,000 in initiatives that will aid in keeping kids safe in class and online. The funding will be used to fight against sex-trafficking, violence against women, and cyberbullying. Examples of the initiatives the government wants to support are WhiteRibbon (to develop program/resources to support boys in secondary school to go against sexual exploitation, violence against women, and attitudes that result in it), and PREVNet (to make resources produced for grades 7-12 to increase knowledge on bullying, harassment, discrimination, in addition to negageing peers to become friends). The Ontario Government wants to protect students through community organizations as mentioned. Feeling welcomed at school creates a positive learning environment for the student and allows them to excel in their studies.

Class Sizes and Course Loads

On that note of bullying and isolation and its impact on learning, one major point Dr. Mardon had mentioned the typical sizes of the classes he was in. Being in a class size of 30-40 students does not do the students justice in a classroom and it is hard to engage all the students in the class. With larger class sizes, teachers can find it hard to recognize difficulties a student may have in class with the course content. Many educators and researchers have agreed that class size does indeed matter (Elementary Teacher Federation of Ontario, n.d.). Large class sizes take away from the focus of letting the students learn and achieve the best to their ability (Elementary Teacher Federation of Ontario, n.d.). A lot of research signifies that smaller class sizes result in more opportunity for an educator to provide students with individual attention (Elementary Teacher Federation of Ontario, n.d.). Smaller class sizes improve student behavior and peer relationships, as well as increase their engagement in early grades (Elementary Teacher Federation of Ontario, n.d.). There is also strong evidence that smaller class sizes benefit students with more educational needs (Elementary Teacher Federation of Ontario, n.d.). This point ties back into Dr. Mardon's case. He mentioned how he needed extra help with writing and the teacher could not support him as much as he had liked. According to Dr. Austin Mardon and the research he had read about 15-16 students per class is the most ideal, rather than in comparison to 40. How many class duration? Class duration is also an important factor to think about when it comes to student learning and engagement. Dr. Mardon believes that there should be more classes in a day but shorter class sizes. Speaking from personal observances, when visiting my old high school during the pandemic in which there were longer class sizes (but only two classes a day in comparison to four shorter ones), students were less engaged with the content and zoned out as a result of it. Various study techniques have used this specific concept/idea. The popular pomodoro method is one that encourages individuals to spend a set short amount of time on a task/subject, such as 25 minutes, then to have a 5 minute break, and then to switch the subject and start the timer again with 25 minutes.

Schooling and getting students ready for the "real world"

Are the courses that elementary and secondary school students really preparing them for the "real world"? There is no doubt that having basic math and literacy skills are crucial to being successful, and in functioning in society and everyday life; however, there are schools covering basic concepts such as mental health, cooking, budgeting/financing, ways to maintain healthy relationships, etc. And where do we draw the line at which schools teach children? And should these topics be put to a higher priority especially with the increased usage of social media by adolescence where they may retain false information? Dr. Mardon agreed that schools should get students more ready for the "real world". For example, he had learned about budgeting in school but not about mortgage. Given that Canada is such a multicultural nation, especially the province of Ontario, many students are children of immigrants who came to Canada and do not understand how to file taxes, the idea of applying for OSAP or other school related funding, and basic banking principles. Dr. Mardon mentioned that it seems important to teach about history, geography, history, classic, rhetoric, as well as creativity. As someone who has recently been in high school myself (specifically in Ontario), I can say that those between grades 9-12 only have to take one geography and history class (geography in grade nine and history in grade ten). And with that being said, there are no classes related to finances or mental health, other than these topics being very briefly touched upon in psychology or business class. On the other hand, one highlight was a food and nutrition class. That class taught those who chose to take it (between grades ten to twelve) what nutrients we need, what the Canadian Food Guide is and how to apply it to our lives, common health concerns that arise due to poor food choices, and to top it all off we got to actually cook some fun meals! Furthermore, Dr. Mardon discusses how attending post secondary is a time of self-discovery. Many students can feel overwhelmed when choosing a career path straight from highschool as one can still have little knowledge on the various fields of study/careers and may not have their own finances ready (to pay off part or the whole amount of tuition/school expenses). Possibly by implementing a finance course, in addition to the others suggested within this section, it could help aid students in getting ready to enter post-secondary, not only mentally, but financially.

Works Cited

https://mppfc.org/
the-importance-of-socialization-in-early-childhood/
https://globalnews.ca/news/7156863/
coronavirus-children-isolation-socialization/

https://www.safecanada.ca/bullying-in-canada/

https://www.redcross.ca/how-we-help/violence-bul-
lying-and-abuse-prevention/educa-
tors/bullying-and-harassment-prevention/
facts-on-bullying-and-harassment

https://news.ontario.ca/en/release/1001824/ontario-strengthen-
ing-protections-against-bullying-and-violence-at-school

https://www.etfo.ca/public-education/class-sizes

Chapter 5:

Graduate school experience, advice for future students, and receiving an honorary doctor of law degree

Written by: Sathurthika Selvanayagam

Dr. Austin Mardon, a former Antarctic researcher, founded the non-profit Canadian charity organisation known as the Antarctic Institute of Canada (AIC) in 1985. The group's initial goal was to influence the federal government of Canada to support more Canadian research in Antarctica. However, AIC slowly diversified and initiated programs for students to publish Antarctic research in newspapers and academic journals. The University of Lethbridge awarded Dr. Mardon, PhD, CM, FRSC, a geography degree in 1985. The next year, at the age of 24, he was a junior field worker on an Antarctic meteorite recovery trip funded by NASA and the National Science Federation, examining meteorite collisions 170 kilometres from the South Pole (Mardon, 2021).

For his efforts, he was awarded the U.S. Antarctic Service Medal. However, the expedition's great challenges had an impact on both his physical and emotional health. His health problems persisted even though he later graduated with master's degrees in science from South Dakota State University and in education from Texas A&M University, and authored a number of books and papers. He was given a schizophrenia diagnosis when he was 30 years old. Dr. Mardon received a PhD in geography from Greenwich University in Australia, continued his impressive record of publication, including articles in Science and Nature, was elected an International Fellow and Corresponding Fellow of the Explorers Club of New York, and was inducted into the International Academy of Astronautics despite the disease limiting some of his abilities (Mardon, 2021).

He was elected into Canada's premier academic society, the Royal Society of Canada, in 2014. His advocacy on behalf of people with mental illnesses has been equally noteworthy. Dr. Mardon has authored essays on faith and schizophrenia, homelessness, medication, and economic support in addition to providing innumerable interviews to the media concerning mental illness. He has served as a leader on the boards of the Schizophrenia Society chapters in Edmonton and Alberta, as well as the Alberta Mental Health Self-Help Network, where he served as coordinator for a period of years. "I hope to soon see the day when schizophrenia is treated like any other disease and is finally detached from the stigma that makes a difficult burden to bear even worse," added Dr. Mardon. Dr. Mardon was recently appointed as an Assistant Adjunct Professor in the University of Alberta Department of Psychiatry, making him the first person with schizophrenia to hold such a position. Dr. Mardon is currently an Assistant

Adjunct Professor with the John Dossetor Health Ethics Centre (Mardon, 2021).

His work for the field of medicine

The Canadian Medical Association (CMA) presented the 2011 CMA Medal of Honour to Dr. Mardon, PhD, for demonstrating outstanding public commitment to raising awareness of mental health issues and diminishing the stigma and discrimination faced by Canadians living with mental illness (Mardon, 2021).

"The CMA Medal of Honour recognizes personal contributions to the advance of medical research and education," said CMA President Dr. Jeff Turnbull. "Dr. Mardon has worked tirelessly to help Canadians better understand the issues around mental illness. In courageously talking openly about his own experiences, he is truly making a difference in coaxing mental illness out of the shadows in this country."

Dr. Mardon Receives Honorary Degree of Doctor of Laws by the University of Alberta

Dr. Mardon, an inspiring advocate for the mentally ill who has worked tirelessly to eliminate the stigma associated with psychiatric disorders, has received an honorary doctor of laws degree during the University of Alberta's 2011 spring convocation ceremonies (Mardon, 2021).

Schooling in Canada reflects the idea of structural functionalism that streaming students is based on merit where the highly capable and hardworking students go into university and others go to the workforce. Moreover, there are many hidden or implicit curricula along with formal education, including concepts such as equity, civil liberty, social rights and the notion that one's success is reflective of their work ethic. For instance the learning that comes from outside of lessons can be very helpful in life and tackling problems later in life. For instance, Dr. Mardon used to play very many board games that always made him to enjoy his education while going through difficult times with his condition. This can be illustrated like playing stimulates brain areas that are responsible for memory formation and complex thought processes for all ages. Engaging in play assists in practicing essential cognitive skills, such as decision making, higher level strategic thinking, and problem solving. This according to Dr. Mardon implies that student should get more experiential learning and experiences outside of school, reflecting their interests. Having to choose a specialization or degree as early as in first year of undergraduate can be less beneficial when it comes to the student not having figured out what their interests are fully yet. He believes that there is more graduate studies, he conversed as how his volunteer experiences and hobbies that he had really taught him life skills that are more than what is needed from a specialization chosen early on in life that is not reflective of one's true wishes. Volunteering can provide a healthy boost to your self-confidence, self-esteem, and life satisfaction. You are doing good for others and the community, which provides a natural sense of accomplishment. Your role as a volunteer can also give you a sense of pride and identity.

He further specified volunteering at a non-profit organization is even beneficial because you get the sense of satisfaction. Moreover volunteering helps create a connnection and feel satisfied at the same time. Often volunteers decide to get involved with NGOs because they want to give back to the community they know and love. It's also an opportunity for people to support community resources that they use themselves, or that they know makes a lot of difference to uplift a community.

Dr. Mardon even mentioned the importance of publishing what you can with your fullest ability. He mentioned that although he was diagnosed with Schizophrenia, he didn't get his meducations until his 30s. But he was able to still publish in 1990 and did research. It builds corporate enthusiasm and supports ongoing education. When you share your published articles internally, it makes others feel proud that they are part of an known and respected organization. Additionally, sharing published pieces with employees helps them better understand marketplace challenges and solutions. He considers being able to publish as giving a very important skill in the growth of someone. In fact, getting published in well-known media outlets is universally recognized as an endorsement or seal of approval.

There are various types of writing, such as creative writing, blogging, narrative writing, journalistic writing, and academic writing. Each writing style has its own set of rules. The primary goal of academic writing is to inform rather than to entertain. Formality, impersonality, structure, and hedging are characteristics (K., 2021). Academic writing must be written in an appropriate and formal language that is not pretentious. A crucial factor to consider is your audience's knowledge and background. You must be able to provide strong and valid references to back up your idea. What is the significance of academic writing? (K., 2021)

Academic writing is essential for success in your working life and career. Most jobs necessitate excellent writing abilities. Most employers place written communication skills at the top of their wish lists. 73% of employers are looking for candidates with strong written communication skills. Aside from leadership and the ability to work well with others, written communication is the most desired overall quality by employers. Great academic writers understand how to effectively communicate by writing about a subject. They simplify things and provide the reader with a broader knowledge and understanding of the subject. When considering the importance of science, technology, and engineering in the educational system, it is recognised that writing is becoming a sought-after skill in the workplace. The Association of American Colleges and Universities conducted a survey in 2013 and discovered that 93% of employers agreed that an employee should be able to think critically, solve complex problems, and communicate clearly. In addition, 75% of employers stated that they want a stronger emphasis on written communication. Writing well can help you succeed in any area of your life. Over a ten-year period, professionals in the employment and recruitment sector who received one to four promotions made 45 percent more grammatical errors than professionals who were promoted six to nine times, according to a grammar study on one hundred Linked in profiles (K., 2021).

Dr. Mardon also mentioned that it is fine to start with a non-academic writing as well. Any publication would be helpful to get you shining in the workplace and make you feel accomplished of having published a work of your what will be appreciated by others. The Internet is the most widely used source for gathering and sharing information. Today, any opinion or fact on any subject is very likely to be found on the internet. Writing articles and posting them on various web-blogs is the most effective way to share your knowledge. Writing and sharing articles has some advantages. One of the most important aspects of article writing is learning and gaining knowledge from the experiences of others. This is the real reason that articles are written and studied. Writing articles allows you to reach out to a global audience and is considered important because readers can accurately relate their experiences and opinions to the content of these articles.

While this isn't ground-breaking career advice, it's crucial. If you have a professional flaw, work on it. Take charge of identifying your skill gaps and working to fill them on a daily basis. After you've resolved one problem, move on to the next. If you're not willing to constantly improve your skill set as a creative professional, you're in the wrong field. It takes passion to succeed in this industry, and without it, your flaws become more apparent as the days pass. Along with improving what you know, it's critical to comprehend what you don't. For example, if you're a web content writer and don't understand why account services is always pushing for more social content, ask them. Learn more about what the client is looking for. It will not only help you deliver more targeted work in the following round, but it will also help you better understand the needs of future clients (Harris, 2020).

Did you overhear in the office that your boss is looking for a writer who is familiar with video game culture? Offer to take on the job. When you can do something that no one else on the team can, such as coding or optimising Web content, you have an undeniable advantage that helps you maintain your position. The more of these "additional benefits" you learn, the more valuable you become as an employee. The bottom line is that if you want to advance in your career, you must be willing to constantly learn, adapt, and improve. We can all benefit from reading more, whether it's bookmarking a few blogs or picking up a new novel by a favourite author. If you limit yourself to a single field or specialty, you will miss out on a (literal) world of information. As a writer, I always benefit from staying current on the industries I write about, which range from finance and healthcare to consumer goods and advertising. You never know when a new piece of information will click and assist you in creating a million-dollar campaign (Harris, 2020).

Non-profits are constantly thinking outside the box about new ideas as they seek solutions to pressing issues in our community. Volunteering at a nonprofit requires you to collaborate, think creatively, and contribute ideas that may have a direct impact on the organization's day-to-day operations. You'll also gain experience problem-solving, teamwork, and working independently. These soft skills will also transfer to other aspects of your life, such as your future studies and career path, as well as your general life. Not only can volunteering at a nonprofit teach you soft skills, but it can also teach you in-depth knowledge about specific topics. Volunteering at a non-profit organisation such as Habitat for Humanity, for example, allows you to learn about affordable housing, construction, and working with various levels of government, among other things. Any nonprofit that focuses on a specific topic will allow you to immerse yourself in that topic. This can be useful for gaining a better understanding of your surroundings, as well as for future studies or career opportunities.

While working at a nonprofit, you will not only learn about a specific area of focus, but you will also learn more about yourself. If you are faced with a difficult situation, learning how to overcome it will provide you with skills to deal with any problems that may arise in the future. Volunteering at a nonprofit will teach you more about the types of work you like and dislike, as well as the larger goals you're capable of achieving when you put your mind to it.

Keeping your mind constantly focused on learning is one of the most beneficial things you can do. This does not imply that you should not concentrate on getting good grades. Grades are merely an aftereffect of learning. Keep an open mind to new experiences and opportunities to apply your knowledge and learn from others. Learning is more than just doing well in class; it is also about being creative and coming up with your own way to contribute.

Schizophrenia is one of the most serious mental illnesses, affecting approximately one in every hundred people over their lifetime. Men and women have different disease outcomes in terms of age of onset, symptoms, disease severity, and number of treatments[1]. Men have a younger onset of the disease, a higher proclivity for negative symptoms, lower social functioning, and co-morbid substance abuse than women, whereas women have a later onset of the disease with more affective symptoms (Li et al., 2016). Dr. Mardon also has mentioned about the sex differences in the prevalence of Schizophrenia among men and women. He mentioned that it is often less likely for men with schizophrenia to be married becasue the social expectations assume that men are meant to be the breadweiners in the family and that they should be the ones providing for the family. However, he is one of those men who got married even though having been diagnosed with Schizophrenia. He also mentioned how the family trends are changing due to the arise in many women working and being the breadwiners in many families. A recent study by Li et al. shows that schizophrenia in men and women are differnet because of many underlying theories, one of wich is the cultural biases as Dr. Mardon has mentioned. Clinical observation reveals that the prevalence, symptoms, and responses to treatment of several psychiatric disorders, including schizophrenia, differ between men and women. While the etiology of gender differences in schizophrenia is only partially understood, recent genetic studies suggest that men and women have distinct sex-specific pathways in schizophrenia. More research is needed to understand the causal roles of gender differences in schizophrenia, with the goal of eventually developing sex-specific treatments for this serious mental illness (Li et al., 2016).Furthermore, because most antipsychotics have side effects, studies have shown that women experienced more of them, including hyperprolactinaemia, hypotension, weight gain, and increased autoimmune proclivity. Women, on the other hand, have higher treatment compliance and better treatment outcomes than men. One of the hypotheses is that women respond better than men to schizophrenia treatment because they have better-preserved social skills. Based on men's and women's responses to schizophrenia treatment, therapy may focus on eliminating substance abuse, developing socio-occupational skills, and reducing negative externalising behaviours in men, while treatment for women may focus on reducing affective symptoms and improving comorbid depression and anxiety (Li et al., 2016).

According to research, there is a significant variation in schizophrenia diagnosis across countries. For example, research by Harrison et al. (1984) suggested that white doctors in Bristol over-diagnosed people of West Indian origin with schizophrenia because of their ethnic background. Furthermore, Copeland et al. (1971) described a patient to 134 US and 194 British psychiatrists. Only 2% of British psychiatrists diagnosed schizophrenia, compared to 69% of US psychiatrists. There has been no research into the cause of this, so it is possible that the symptoms of ethnic minorities are misinterpreted. This calls the reliability of schizophrenia diagnosis into question because it implies that patients can exhibit the same symptoms but receive different diagnoses due to their ethnic background; i.e., a patient's ethnicity makes it more or less likely that they will be diagnosed with schizophrenia (Schizophrenia: Culture n.d).

According to Dr. Mardon, one of the important ways to do better in graduate school even if there are underlying stigma, would be to increase the amount of people that you are with and increase the friends circle. Peer support can have an impact on overall academic development, knowledge acquisition, and self-esteem. Having valuable college friendships during your undergraduate or graduate career can lead to an improved social life, a successful and fulfilling education, and sought-after career opportunities. Emotion is important in the educational experience. Faculty and staff can assist students in developing friendships by cultivating a community culture — both physically and virtually.Professionals in postsecondary education must ensure that students have inclusive and psychologically safe spaces. Together, faculty and staff can find solutions by teaching the curricula as their authentic selves and inviting students to search within and support the same sentiments (Friday, 2021).

Thus, Dr. Mardon always be a role model and a living example for showing how important it is to have a life outside of academia which would not only help one success academically but also in one's life as an individual. It is important to focus on the career without compromisting the personal growth as a good citizen. By building a network outside of school through volunteering, playing games, wiring and publishing articles and research papers, collaborating with others as well as venturing and exploring outside of comfort zone, one can deal with change—and making change in a much better way.

References

Friday, V. (2021, May 27). *The importance of friendship for college students.* Goodwin University.

Retrieved November 29, 2022, from https://www.goodwin.edu/ enews/friendship-and-the-life-and-longevity-of-college-learn- ers/#:~:text=Supportive%20interactions%20with%20peers%20 can,and%20sought%2Dafter%20career%20opportunities.

Harris, S. (2020, December 22). *Why volunteer at a nonprofit?* Habitat for Humanity

Halton-Mississauga. Retrieved November 29, 2022, from https://habitathm.ca/volunteer-nonprofit-habitat/#:~:text=Volunteering%20at%20a%20nonprofit%20means,a%20team%20and%20working%20independently.

K., U. (2021, November 23). *Importance of academic writing.* LinkedIn. Retrieved November 29,

2022, from https://www.linkedin.com/pulse/importance-academic-writing-uvaldi-kleynhans/?trk=public_profile_article_view

Li, R., Ma, X., Wang, G., Yang, J., & Wang, C. (2016, September). *Why sex differences in*

schizophrenia? Journal of translational neuroscience. Retrieved November 29, 2022, from https://www.ncbi.nlm.nih.gov/pmc/articles/PMC5688947/

Mardon, A. (2021, January 29). *Home.* Austin Mardon. Retrieved November 29, 2022, from

https://austinmardon.org/

Schizophrenia: Culture. tutor2u. (n.d.). Retrieved November 29, 2022, from

https://www.tutor2u.net/psychology/reference/schizophrenia-culture

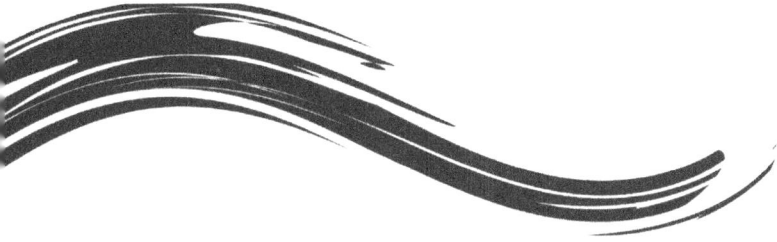

Section Three:

COVID-19 Impact

Chapter 6:

Spearheading new initiatives during the pandemic

Written by: Noah Varghese

Introduction

Who is Dr. Austin Mardon?

If anyone were to ask the question, "Who is Dr. Austin Mardon?" several answers could be given, but none would do the professor justice. Born in Edmonton, Alberta, Canada, Dr. Mardon pursued a major in cultural geography at the University of Lethbridge in Canada. She would continue his studies as a graduate student at South Dakota State University. He would eventually secure several degrees, including a master's in education, a Ph. D, and even an honorary Law Degree. Hearing this alone should indicate that Dr. Mardon is, first and foremost, an educator who will play a significant role during the pandemic. He has also advocated for exploring different teaching and learning styles in Canada, as he remembered in detail how the education system failed to accommodate his different skillset. Even before the pandemic, he was already working towards changing the traditional work environment. Even though he volunteers as an adjunct professor, he is still recognized for his contributions to education, such as being awarded the Order of Canada for his contributions to education. This wasn't the only award he obtained for his contributions to education, nor his last.

If unsatisfied with the description of an educator, you will be happy to know Dr. Mardon's accomplishments don't stop there. Many would also describe him as scientifically curious, someone who would go to great lengths to learn and explore new academic fields. To get a sense of his explorative nature, one of his notable accomplishments is his NASA-sponsored venture to the Antarctic for a meteorite expedition. This nature was responsible for his contributions to historical astronomy, where he ventured through the ancient Anglo-Saxon Chronicles and identified several cometary events never mentioned in other texts. His commitment to scientific exploration fueled several of the projects he took on during the pandemic.

Dr. Mardon can also be described as a strong advocate for mental health. Ever since he was diagnosed with schizophrenia, he has been open about the illness and strived to challenge its stigma. His work with the Alberta Mental Health Self-Help network as the coordinator ensures that the local community has access to helpful resources, especially when the illness is not well understood. The Canadian Medical Health Association and Alberta Medical Association recognized his contributions. His understanding of the foreseeable decline in mental health among students during the pandemic was a solid reason to start his COVID-19 initiatives.

Finally, and perhaps most significant in the context of his pandemic initiatives, Dr. Mardon was known to be a writer. Along with his family, he is known to the author, co-authored, edited, and published over 50 books in several fields. Either advocating for mental health, diving into history, or even dabbling in children's literature and nonfiction. Unfortunately, even though he retains his passion for writing and publishing, his mental and physical health ailments prevent him from writing as frequently as he would like.

Publishing Before the Pandemic

As mentioned previously, Dr. Mardon is an avid writer and is well known for publishing his or his student's work with several agencies. For example, he frequently publishes with the Golden Meteorite Press, a publishing company started by his wife, Catherine Mardon, and himself. Golden Meteorite Press is a well-equipped company that features several books from genres like Canadian Politics, Fiction, Geography and Wayfinding, Health and well-being, History, and Science and Nature. These books were also published in several international languages, including but not limited to Bengali, German, Vietnamese, and Arabic. Additionally, several books, even with the limited staff, were translated into other languages for many indigenous communities in Canada, like "Gandy and the Man in White." All of the books can be found on the goldenmeteoritepress.com website or can be purchased on Lulu.

Given his kind nature, he has made a good portion of his publications freely available on the website Academia.edu, aligning with his philosophy of serving as a mentor for the community. Before the pandemic, most of his publications were geared towards advocating for mental health and elaborating on his experiences with schizophrenia or the available mental health services. For example, in 2009, Dr. Mardon detailed his personal story with schizophrenia to accomplish three objectives. Firstly, to educate the general population about schizophrenia. Secondly, to advocate for more investment into the treatment of the illness, given that his poster mentions significant side effects of the current medication that impairs his day-to-day life. Finally, this poster aims to decrease the stigma surrounding schizophrenia by demonstrating that despite the challenges Dr. Mardon encountered, he still completed his Ph.D., is still a recognized educator in the community and received several national, including one directly from the governor-general, Michelle Jean. The published poster is "Growing Older with Schizophrenia: The Personal Story of Austin Mardon."

It would be unjust not to mention Catherine Mardon, Dr. Mardon's wife when discussing his projects before the pandemic. Like Dr. Mardon, Catherine Mardon has a prestigious academic background where she studied for a Juris Doctor and received a master's degree in theological studies. Her passion, similar to that of Dr. Mardon, is also being a social advocate, especially for the homeless, a demographic that overlaps with those inflicted with mental illness. In 1991, she was attacked and left for dead for her involvement in a testimony against a white supremacist group. This tragedy left her with PTSD and traumatic brain injury limiting her work as a lawyer. However, she has shifted her focus to advocating for the disabled, like her husband, and to writing literature, especially children's books. Before the pandemic, she and her husband have written several children's books, many of which are part of the "Gandy" series, which follows the titular character on his adventures interacting with different environments, professions, and animals. Catherine Mardon is Dr. Mardon's most frequent and most significant collaborator regarding book publishing.

The second group that most collaborates with Dr. Mardon is students, although infrequently. As he aged, Dr. Mardon has found himself finding less time and capability to write and publish as many books as decades ago, even when he was brimming with ideas. His solution was to employ university students, using a portion of his disability grant given by the Ontario Government and other services, to write novels about topics he desired. For example, the earliest book written by a student under the tutelage of Dr. Mardon was by Jagdeep Gill, titled "Life after a Bachelor's: A Guide to the Options Available to Recent College Graduates." Dr. Mardon would often employ Albertan students during the summer, given that writing books or chapters can be very exhausting, especially when balancing classes. However, the caveat of this schedule is that Dr. Mardon worked with a limited number of students before the pandemic.

Surprisingly, the group Dr. Mardon worked with the least was other scholars and professors in his field. Although he has published and presented at scientific or mental health-related conferences, he has commented that the stigma around his schizophrenia was the main barrier behind most interactions. The scientific meetings he attended were over a decade ago, the most recent being the Lunar and Planetary Scientific Conference in 2010 in Houston Texas. He presented his research project on trends in world metal consumption and the eventual need to invest in mining for minerals in space or at least from meteorites. Leading up to the pandemic, Dr. Mardon has shifted his focus to advocacy in mental health and away from his academia in meteorology and cultural geography. This includes presenting at conferences or meetings held by the University of Alberta, where he details his history with mental health. He rarely travels to other universities for his presentations and rarely interacts with other professors at these conferences, but instead with other mental health advocates.

Activity during the Pandemic
Initial Reaction to the Pandemic

When the pandemic hit and the threat of job loss loomed over many students, there was a fear held by every one of how the economy would be impacted in the long term, Dr. Mardon included. But Dr. Mardon was also concerned about the toll of potential social isolation on his physical and mental health. He struggled with obesity, like many other people with schizophrenia, and was fearful of how the pandemic might force an unhealthy sedentary lifestyle. Additionally, social isolation can limit other patients with schizophrenia from seeking treatment or daily contact with loved ones. As a result, there was a lot of uncertainty regarding how to The pandemic forced many to adopt a more sedentary lifestyle, which was a fear for Dr. Mardon. Additionally, income became scarcer for the Mardon family and they, like many other people across Canada, were concerned about how to make ends meet. Finally, Dr. Mardon feared that many of his students who were writing and researching might not be able to publish when the pandemic arrived in Canada. He was correct since the restrictions interfered with, delayed, or completely halted many projects, especially those run by undergraduate students. He immediately worked with his students to arrange a publication with several peer-reviewed journals to resolve this.

Before the pandemic, the plan was to continue holding summer grants for students, especially those interested in writing and needing financial assistance. However, the pandemic changed that for multiple reasons. Firstly, the coming of the pandemic also shifted technology, specifically the dependence on technology. Dr. Mardon wasn't "computer-illiterate," but completely changing one's habits, means of communication, and writing process to accommodate the rapid digitalization is not easy, as many professors can relate. Even when managing and creating several projects, he was overwhelmed with mentoring and guiding more students than he had ever worked with before and learning how to navigate new technology to communicate with several hundred people. He had to shift his role from a writer to a leader, publisher, and editor. He has commented that he could continue managing the project thanks to his wife, Catherine Mardon, and some of his students. Because of their help, the projects he started during the pandemic are as big as they are today.

Initial start to the COVID-19 Projects

During the pandemic, Dr. Mardon was made known across Canada for his writing initiatives designed to help students become better writers. He has accomplished this project through several mediums, but primarily through Riipen LevelUP, Venture, Sharpen the Quill (his organization), and Canada Summer Jobs. Riipen was a relatively new initiative based in British Columbia that connected students with organizations to gain work experience remotely. It was founded by students and was responsible for distributing funding to many of these work/volunteer projects. Since their goals of education and providing students with hands-on experience even during the pandemic aligned with Dr. Mardon's goals in the past decade, Dr. Mardon received 1.6 million Canadian dollars in funding in his first year of the project. Likewise, Canada Summer Jobs also provided $340,000 to Dr. Mardon in the first year. Dr. Mardon owes their huge initial grant in part since his history with working with students was readily available online, and he was, in his own words, "an open book." Regardless of the organization, the task and objective remained the same: provide topics and opportunities for students to research and write and improve their writing skills in whatever field they pursue.

Although these COVID-19 projects sound similar to the previous projects that Dr. Mardon hosted years before, these projects are very different in execution. The significant difference is that the scale is far more extensive. Dr. Mardon worked with Canada

Summer Jobs to secure more funding to take in more students, specifically over 500 students in the project's first year. The number of participating students only increased in the following years. Unlike previous projects, the student demographic was also widely different than before. In addition to having a wider distribution of students across the country, most students had a pre-med or life sciences background. His explanation for this change is that many life science students lost their internships and jobs in the health sector because of the pandemic. This led to a surge of students looking for remote opportunities, where they eventually stumbled upon the Antarctic Institute of Canada. The demographic change impacted the mode of communication, the need to delegate tasks to team leaders (who are also other students), and to identify topics that interest the public. Additionally, adding more students allowed students to be responsible for only writing chapters collaboratively instead of whole books individually.

Even though the first year of the project was successful, Dr. Mardon encountered several challenges that weren't as prevalent in his previous project. As mentioned before, managing the 500 students was a nightmare and only possible thanks to Catherine Mardon and other experienced students who were responsible for taking on some of the responsibility. Catherine Mardon was incredibly influential in the project in helping publish and edit. Her specialty lies in her ability to determine if what the students wrote won't cause any legal problems later on. For example, several students were noted to be controversial in their chapters, such as writing opinionated pieces about current politicians or plagiarizing materials. In both cases, and more, Catherine and Austin Mardon carefully edited out these pieces while maintaining the rest of the chapter. Another challenge encountered was an abundance of writers, but not enough graphic designers to create book covers. Alternatively, some students would include questionable content that would not synergize with the rest of the book's content. It was the couple's responsibility to ensure that there wasn't any odd chapter or piece that tarnished or reflected poorly on the rest of the book and co-authors. Dr. Mardon found it extremely difficult to find students who had experience designing art or book covers and a passion for doing it for books written by "amateur writers."

Growths of the Projects
As the projects progressed, several changes took place to either accommodate the students, the funding agencies, and for the readers. For the students, the duration and pace of the project shifted based on what the student was comfortable with. For example, some projects would last a couple of weeks, while others would last 2 months. Dr. Mardon implemented this to accommodate better students and their busy schedules especially given how unpredictable the pandemic lockdown could be. Additionally, at the beginning of the second year, new roles were available for students apart from being a book author and a graphic designer. Specifically, some students were tasked with either previous translating publications into many other languages. Other students worked with audio recording, acting as audio engineers or audiobook readers to make some of Dr. Mardon's most famous texts readily available. Another way the project changed was that Dr. Mardon created a conference and event to celebrate other students' completion of their projects. Students proud of their time with

the Antarctic Institute of Canada, either through Riipen, Venture, Canada Summer Jobs, or any other medium, can present their work in the annual August conference. The conference does not provide any monetary award but allows students to network with other student authors and receive certification as proof that they contributed to the Antarctic Institute of Canada.

An unintended side effect of many students taking on the project was that students who started applying for the grant regularly began to network with Dr. Austin and other mature students. Specifically, Dr. Mardon started to serve as a mentor regarding mental health and career prospects. Many students were burdened by financial complications, academic obligations, and trauma from how the pandemic affected them. His experience as an advocate was useful in recommending resources for students based on what they were going through, but he was also a compassionate listener. As a professor, he was also sage about career paths in medicine, law, and other fields. Increasingly, he would talk to students for hours on end, advising them on planning their undergraduate/ graduate careers. In this way, the Antarctic Institute of Canada was not only an organization that gathered students together who were keen on learning writing but also a medium for Dr. Mardon to continue serving as a mental health and student advisor.

Conclusion

The pandemic has been hectic and technically ongoing, but that hasn't stopped Dr. Mardon's efforts to continue improving the project, even now. His work was instrumental in providing the next generation of employees entering the workforce with invaluable experience as writers. Additionally, his time with the students provided financial assistance to many left unemployed students and mentorship to those who had questions about career prospects and healthy mental health maintenance. His contributions weren't unrecognized, as he was awarded several titles, such as The IIPL Peace and Cultural Award, the AAG Diversity and Inclusion Award, and the Zimbabwe Academy of Sciences Fellowship.

Reflection

When asked about his thoughts on the program and the outcome in the last 2 years, Dr. Mardon commented that he was constantly impressed with the perseverance of many students. Their eagerness to learn under strenuous circumstances and create work in a short amount of time surprised him. Looking back, he wished he could reach out to more students from diverse backgrounds, not only as authors but as audio engineers and graphic designers. Additionally, he was already very proud of some of the student's chapters, especially when they were cited in other publications. For example, "Understanding Music," a book authored by Dr. Mardon, Kyra Droog, Alyssa Kulchisky, has been mentioned several times. Given that this book has been one of the first publications in the Canadian Summer Job cohort during the pandemic, he is optimistic that more novels will be cited in time. Finally, if there is one thing to be thankful for when organizing these projects, it is that his digital literacy improved significantly. He is now very comfortable using Zoom, and other digital communication platforms, enabling him to connect with more students and peers across Canada. Although this pandemic has been hard for everyone, Dr. Mardon's expertise in publishing has been helpful for students across Canada in learning to be better writers.

Chapter 7:

Overcoming challenges

Written by: Wan Ling Dai

Challenges Before the COVID-19 Pandemic

Coming to Terms with Diagnosis

Prior to the onset of the coronavirus disease 2019 (COVID-19) pandemic, Austin faced many challenges, some of which stemmed from his schizophrenia diagnosis. After receiving this diagnosis, Austin took a lot of time to accept this illness. When he was initially diagnosed with schizophrenia, many of his friends and family reacted in fear of Austin and he began to lose contact with those friends and family members. Austin began to isolate himself as he felt that he had nothing in common with others and there was usually an awkward silence when he tried to converse with his friends. But through his journey to accept his illness, he gained a greater sense of freedom as he began to understand his limitations. This realisation of his limitations allowed him to discover and appreciate the freedoms that he still had. These limitations included giving up driving, never being able to pay back his student loans, likely never working a full-time job and instead, having to live on a modest income. By accepting his mental illness and being aware of these limitations, Austin felt more confident and comfortable going out into public areas and understanding what activities he could participate in.

Living A Fulfilling Life

One of the struggles of having a disruptive mental illness, like schizophrenia, is pursuing a life packed with fulfilment. People with mental disorders tend to lose some of the luxuries of life that individuals without mental disorders have. But individuals with schizophrenia can still live an enjoyable life. Austin, alongwith his wife, were able to retire at an early age, normally an age when people would be beginning their careers. Austin and his wife had to live a modest life and make do with what they had. Despite Austin being retired and unable to work a job, he continued to do various fulfilling activities with his life. To keep himself moving forward in life and inspire him to complete new goals, Austin completed a lot of volunteer work. For example, one of the first things he did when he left the hospital was going to a schizo-phrenia self support group, known as "Unsung Heroes", where later, he earned himself the position of co-Chairman. He also began to volunteer at the Clubhouse Society of Edmonton which is an organisation that assists individuals with mental disorders express themself using various different forms of media. For all his volunteer work, in November 1997, Austin was awarded the Governor General's Caring Canadian Award which he regards as one of the greatest honours of his life and serves as a powerful motivation to continue to strive for success. All the volunteer work that Austin had completed filled a gap in his life that his diagnosis had created. Volunteer work is suitable for everyone and can be an extremely beneficial way for individuals with mental illnesses to build a worthwhile experience and ease themselves into feeling comfortable in new environments.

Managing Finances Successfully

Another major struggle that accompanies individuals with mental disorders is financial management because these individuals are usually limited in their career opportunities. Many of the limitations in career advancement that schizophrenics face are due to the stigma and misconceptions associated with schizophrenia. One of the best methods to manage one's finances successfully is to utilise a budget. A budget helps prevent one from making unnecessary purchases and showcase the allocation of one's money. A useful budget would be to have several sub-divisions, namely the following sections: monthly income, monthly fixed expenses, daily expenses, obligations and desires (Mardon et al., 2010, p. 31-36).

Trying to Live Independently

Having a support system, such as family, is the strongest wall for a person with mental illness to lean on. Family members usually display protective behaviour for their loved ones, which results in a kind of care and attention that makes individuals with mental disorders feel loved and supported during difficult times. However, this results in these individuals becoming dependent on their family members for support. Being dependent on others is not necessarily a bad thing, it is important for people with schizophrenia to have the ability to talk to someone. Otherwise, they would isolate themselves and feel unwelcome in society. Nevertheless, being able to be independent is something that everyone wants from a young age. Being able to make one's own decisions and complete tasks on one's own is something people yearn for as they grow from the adolescent years to their adulthood. For an individual without a mental illness, independence may be in the form of moving to a new city, living alone and having their own source of income; essentially being able to make their own choices and learn from their mistakes without being controlled by a higher authority. But for an individual with a mental illness, independence can be defined as the ability to perform a task without the assistance of a caretaker or another person (Mardon et al., 2010, p. 48). So even a small task, such as cooking oneself a meal, would be considered a significant accomplishment. Learning to complete these tasks requires a lot of time and repetition; however the feeling of satisfaction and accomplishment motivates mentally ill patients to continue to work harder to build their independence. Additionally, by building a patient's independence, they will begin to feel a larger sense of normality and feel more belongingness in society. This is also beneficial to help patients feel more comfortable being left alone in settings with a large number of people. However, independence for mentally ill patients must also be brought about by altering the way society views individuals with mental illness. Having society becoming more accepting of patients with mental health disorders allows them to gain more confidence and build a world that is more accessible for these patients.

Importance of Medication

Austin attributes his medication as his key to being able to live a thriving life with a mental illness. Following his initial diagnosis, Austin would not comply with the medical staff to take his medication, which is a common occurrence among many schizophrenics with only about 5 percent of all schizophrenics actually complying and taking their medication (Mardon et al., 2010, p. 16). He believed that the medications he was given was a method for the medical staff to poison him. This resulted in the doctor calling Austin's father and requesting him to talk to Austin. After having spoken to his father for three hours, Austin was persuaded and has never failed to take his medication since. In addition, Austin was able to find a physician that he was able to develop a healthy relationship with built upon understanding, trust and familiarity. Another reason Austin continually takes his medication is that he has seen schizophrenics end up living on the streets as a result of not taking their medicine properly (Mardon et al., 2010, p. 42). Austin also mentioned that individuals diagnosed with schizophrenia who do not take their medication are endangering themselves and putting their family through misery as 40 percent of schizophrenics will attempt suicide and 10 percent are successful in doing so (Mardon et al., 2010, p. 43). Hence, Austin understood the importance of taking his medications and the suggestions of his doctor.

Overcoming the Stigma and Misconceptions of Mental Illness

Oftentimes people have negative perceptions of individuals with mental health illnesses. The stigma that mental illness patients face varies depending on the people they are interacting with.

Society often views mentally ill patients as people who are unable to function and may alienate these patients because they are seen as dangerous. Other misconceptions that exist about individuals with schizophrenia include that it is untreatable, it worsens with time and schizophrenics speak nothing except nonsense (Mardon et al., 2010, p. 57). These misconceptions lead the general public to believe schizophrenic patients are insane. However, family members of an individual with schizophrenia produce a different type of stigma from that of strangers. Parents of a schizophrenic patient tend to be overprotective of their child due to society's belief that schizophrenics are unable to function on their own. The restriction of the child's freedom may result in the child becoming reliant on their parent which hinders the ability for the schizophrenic patient to be independent (Mardon et al., 2010, p. 60). Additionally, families of patients diagnosed with schizophrenia are often stigmatised due to being associated with someone that society deems as insane. Austin recalls in his childhood after his mother was diagnosed with schizophrenia, other students, parents of those students and church goers would make fun of him (Mardon et al., 2010, p. 61). For Austin, he was able to overcome the judgements he received from other people and focus on other things that were important to him.

Challenges During and After the COVID-19 Pandemic

The COVID-19 sent the entire globe into an immediate shutdown. Many individuals were forced to stay in their homes to help prevent the spread of the virus. For many, this quarantine was challenging - having to face a long period of isolation for the first time. In a study completed at the University of Warsaw, the five greatest challenges that participants faced were the limitations of direct contact with people, restrictions on movements and travel, change in active lifestyle, boredom and monotony, and finally uncertainty about the future (Maison et al., 2021). Dr. Austin Mardon is certainly no stranger to these challenges - having faced similar difficulties during the COVID-19 pandemic.

Transitioning to a Remote Workplace

When the COVID-19 pandemic forced everyone into quarantine, it in turn forced everyone to adopt a new daily routine. Many services and businesses had to adopt practices to be able to operate remotely; an example being conducting virtual meetings instead of in-person meetings. Austin initially faced the technological and social challenge of this switch to remote work. This was a common occurrence for many people that switched to working remotely. Many employees had to learn how to use new collaboration platforms and digital working tools. Additionally, these employees had to combine their working hours with their personal and family commitments which resulted in many people feeling as though there was no separation between work and life. Austin had felt this during the pandemic as he was working home and receiving more phone calls on a daily basis. In addition to having many daily video meetings, employees were feeling more isolated without the normal face to face interactions they would experience in an office. Despite that, many individuals found that working remotely allowed them more time for other activities as remote work eliminated the daily commute time employees had to previously take. The loss of daily social interaction was something that Austin had felt during the COVID-19 quarantine. However, with this new way to conduct meetings during these isolated times, Austin was able to work with more students across the country and internationally instead of only collaborating with students in Alberta.

Mental Health During the COVID-19 Pandemic

Along with many other individuals, the quarantine had an impact on Austin's mental health. In an interview, Austin mentioned feeling depressed as the quarantine progressed. This was a common feeling for many people staying at home due to the pandemic. In an article by the World Health Organization (WHO), in the first year of the COVID-19 pandemic, the prevalence of anxiety and depression had triggered a 25 percent increase across the globe (World Health Organization, 2022). The major reason for this spike in the prevalence of anxiety and depression is the result from the isolation that many individuals were experiencing. Prior to the COVID-19 pandemic, some people struggled to receive mental health treatments due to barriers such as shortage of accessible mental health professionals, lack of mental health service integration and government oversight, and cost of services not covered by private insurance plans (Moroz et al., 2020). Hence with this large increase in mental health issues brought on by the pandemic, it became even more challenging to receive the needed care for those who need it most. Austin stated that he felt that this is one issue that individuals with mental health conditions struggled with the most. For those who were receiving mental health treatments before the COVID-19 quarantine, it was difficult to transition from face-to-face care to online support as the online support lacked the emotional and social aspect that came along with an in person session.

When looking back on life before the pandemic, Austin discussed how he used to be more of a social butterfly. However, as the quarantine wore on and virtual meetings became more of the norm, Austin recalls how he lost a lot of friends and people within his social network. This was a common occurrence for many people during the COVID-19 pandemic after having experienced such a long period of loneliness and isolation. In a study done at the University of Sydney with more than 2,000 participants, some findings were that particular groups of people were more vulnerable to losing friends, including singles or those with social anxiety, and mental disabilities (Black, 2022).

Government Assistance During the Quarantine

During the unprecedented times of the COVID-19 pandemic, there were many factors and decisions that the Canadian government had to address in order to support its citizens. With such an increase in the presence of mental health problems, it was important that the Canadian government set up some initiatives to reduce the feeling of stress, anxiety and depression among Canadians during a time of isolation. In April 2020, the Government of Canada along with Stepped Care Solutions, Kids Help Phone, and Homewood Health launched Wellness Together Canada (WTC) (Government of Canada, 2022). WTC is an online platform that allows users access to a virtual network of mental health and substance use support. As of January 10, 2022, over two million people from across all the provinces and territories have accessed the WTC portal, with 20,000 to 30,000 using the services on the WTC portal on a weekly basis (Government of Canada, 2022). In order to make the WTC portal more accessible, the Government of Canada launched the PocketWell App which is a mobile platform that connects to the WTC portal and makes it easier for people to identify, understand and access free and confidential mental health and substance use services (Government of Canada, 2022). As beneficial as these services are, Austin had mentioned that rural areas needed more government support. Since the COVID-19 pandemic required many non-essential services be switched to a virtual platform, this also required people to have access to the internet. While 98.6 per cent of individuals living in urban areas do have internet access, only 45.6 per cent of Canadians living in rural areas have access to the internet and First Nations reserves have even less with only 34.8 percent of households having access to the internet (Zarum, 2022). So, despite the Canadian government launching an online platform to support Canadians, the platform is not accessible to all citizens. In addition, due to the lack of internet access in rural areas, many communities suffered outages for weeks at a time as a result of schooling and health care transitioning to a virtual setting. The federal government has recognized the importance of providing internet access to rural communities and First Nation reserves by promising to connect 98 percent of Canadians to high-speed internet by 2026 and 100 percent by 2030 (Zarum, 2022). Austin believes more could have been done by the government earlier to support Canadians living in rural communities during the quarantine.

New Career Changes

The sudden presence of the COVID-19 pandemic altered the lives of many with many people deciding new goals for their lives. One such change is deciding a new step in one's career. For Austin, the COVID-19 pandemic has allowed him to focus more on working with students. During the pandemic, he began taking his work with the Antarctic Institute of Canada (AIC) onto the Riipen platform. Riipen is a platform that allows employers to post industry related projects that Canadian post-secondary students can complete to help equip them with work-ready skills and help them advance in their careers. Riipen's Level UP program is also in part funded by the Government of Canada's Innovative Work-Integrated Learning (I-WIL) Initiatives program which was developed to help give Canadian post-secondary students an opportunity to gain valuable and relevant work experience. This platform has allowed Austin to meet and work with students across the country as he previously was only working with students based in Edmonton. After being able to work with students from different provinces and territories, Austin has mentioned wanting to work with students across the world and he wished it was something he pursued earlier, especially with video conferencing platforms, such as Zoom and Microsoft Teams, making long distance meetings significantly simpler.

Outlook on Life After the COVID-19 Pandemic

When the COVID-19 pandemic first began, some people viewed it as the end of the world. All non-essential businesses were closed and people were stuck in their homes. Some people felt as though their life was put on pause. For many, it was an awakening to how short life can be and how important it is to live life to the fullest. That was especially the case for Austin. After having lived through a pandemic, he viewed it as a wake up call. Austin felt this experience allowed him to focus more on him and learn more about what makes him happier and enjoy life more. A lesson Austin learned from the COVID-19 pandemic experience is that life is short and as the COVID-19 pandemic has proven, everything can change so suddenly. So everyone should enjoy the most out of life and find activities that make life feel fulfilling. He also felt that a person should not be constantly on a grind their entire life and it is better to take some time off to relax and enjoy one's life. It is especially important that individuals find happiness within their lives and continue to always be happy.

References

Black, S. (2022, January 2). *Why 'pruning' friends has been so common during the pandemic.* The Guardian. Retrieved November 22, 2022, from https://www.theguardian.com/lifeandstyle/2022/jan/03/why-pruning-friends-has-been-so-common-during-the-pandemic

Government of Canada. (2022, March 24). *Government of Canada improves digital access to mental health and substance use resources during the covid-...* Canada.ca. Retrieved November 22, 2022, from https://www.canada.ca/en/health-canada/news/2022/01/government-of-canada-improves-digital-access-to-mental-health-and-substance-use-resources-during-the-covid-19-

pandemic.html

Maison D, Jaworska D, Adamczyk D, Affeltowicz D (2021) The challenges arising from the COVID-19 pandemic and the way people deal with them. A qualitative longitudinal study. PLoS ONE 16(10): e0258133. https://doi.org/10.1371/journal.pone.0258133

Mardon, A. A., Sivakumar, M., Sivakumar, M., Gill, N., & Gill, G. (2010). Thriving with schizophrenia. Golden Meteorite Press.

Moroz N, Moroz I, D'Angelo MS. (2020, July 2). Mental health services in Canada: Barriers and cost-effective solutions to increase access. Healthcare Management Forum. 2020;33(6):282-287. doi:10.1177/0840470420933911

World Health Organization. (2022, March 2). Covid-19 pandemic triggers 25% increase in prevalence of anxiety and depression worldwide. World Health Organization. Retrieved November 22, 2022, from https://www.who.int/news/item/02-03-2022-covid-19-pandemic-triggers-25-increase-in-prevalence-of-anxiety-and-depression-worldwide

Zarum, D. (2022, February 14). *Rural internet could hold the key to Canada's economic future.* CPA Canada. Retrieved November 22, 2022, from https://www.cpacanada.ca/en/news/pivot-magazine/2021-02-14-rural-internet

Section 4:

Conversation Topics

Chapter 8:

Finding inspiration and motivation in an ever-changing world

Written by: Suhaib Aldada

Motivation is a force that seems to be necessary for achieving a goal. This force can motivate someone to act in a specific way in order to achieve the desired outcome. All living creatures have motivation, a powerful force that propels people and shapes their conduct (Amernic & Craig, 2019). A need is the first step in the internal process of motivation. An individual's motivation is sparked by this desire, shaping how they behave to fulfill the need. A person's motivation is an internal drive which pushes or pulls them to behave in a particular way rather than a behavior that may be forced upon them (Plouffe, 2017). An individual may eventually lose motivation because it is not a skill that can be sustained on an ongoing basis. The inability to muster the willpower to carry out one's wishes is a sign of someone who lacks motivation. The main determinant of someone's failure or success is whether they are motivated or not. However, by looking for sources of inspiration and motivation outside the traditional places, they can find the drive they need to pursue their goals (Locke & Latham, 2019). For example, when one is feeling lost, he or she can look to nature for guidance.

The world is constantly changing and evolving. What was once new and exciting can quickly become old and stale. It can be difficult to find inspiration and motivation when the world around one is constantly changing (Amernic & Craig, 2019). However, there are ways to find inspiration and motivation in an ever-changing world. One way to find inspiration and motivation is to set goals. Having something to strive for can give one a much-needed sense of purpose. It can be easy to lose sight of one's goals if the world around one is constantly changing. However, it can be easier to find inspiration and motivation if one has a clear goal.

Furthermore, setting goals helps obtain motivation and inspiration by providing a clear and attainable target to work towards. Having a specific goal in mind can help focus one's efforts and give one a sense of purpose (Plouffe, 2017). Seeing the progress one makes toward their goal can also be a great source of motivation and inspiration. Therefore, finding inspiration and motivation can be difficult in an ever-changing world.

Another way to find inspiration and motivation is to connect with others. There is strength in numbers. If one feels like they are the only one struggling to find inspiration and motivation, reach out to others (Amernic & Craig, 2019). There are likely others who feel the same way. Connecting with others can help them realize that they are not alone. Therefore one of the best ways to find inspiration is to connect with others who are creative and have a similar passion. When people connect with others, we can share ideas, experiences, and resources that can help us be more creative and productive (Plouffe, 2017). Additionally, being around others who are creative can help to spark new ideas and help us to think outside the box.

If the world around one is constantly changing, it is important to find a way to change. One way to do this is to find inspiration and motivation from within. Everyone has the ability to find inspiration and motivation within themselves (Amernic & Craig, 2019). It may take some time to find it, but it is there. Some people find inspiration and motivation from within by looking to their values and setting goals that are in line with those values. Others may find inspiration and motivation from within by taking on new challenges and pushing themselves outside their comfort levels (Plouffe, 2017). Still, others may find inspiration and motivation from within by connecting with nature, spending time with loved ones, or engaging in creative pursuits. Ultimately, there is no single answer to this question, and what works for one person may not work for another. It can be difficult to find inspiration and motivation in an ever-changing world. However, it is possible. Start with the aforementioned ideas of setting goals, connecting with others, and finding inspiration and motivation from within. These three things can help one find inspiration and motivation in an ever-changing world.

There are several ways to get motivated. Emotional, biological, environmental, psychological, and evolutionary factors are among them. Scientists concentrate more on individuals' intrinsic and extrinsic dispositions to comprehend how motivation influences an individual. A person's inner self is where intrinsic drive originates. It is a human urge to find contentment in oneself (Bird & Mendenhall, 2017). When someone is intrinsically driven, they feel compelled to do a task because completing it makes them happy or they just like doing it. Scientists assess a person's interest to gauge their level of satisfaction while carrying out specific tasks to quantify intrinsic motivation. Another approach is a behavioral approach, which involves observing how a person accomplishes tasks under various circumstances (Plouffe, 2017).

An outside influence is the source of extrinsic motivation. It is the desire for benefits or inducements. These honors or rewards might come in cash, gifts, medals, promotions, or elevated social prestige (Plouffe, 2017). Extrinsically motivated people may execute tasks they loathe in order to get the desired outcome. Many people use extrinsic motivation for a variety of reasons. Depending on the job being performed and the confidence level of the individual performing the work, it might create varying levels of arousal. The reward received boosts one's sense of value and encourages the individual's conduct.

Extrinsic motivation encourages someone to carry out duties even when tempted to quit. The effects of extrinsic motivation can be either favorable or harmful. Extrinsic motivation has advantages since it enables people to create objectives and accomplish the actions required to get the desired reward (Pink, 2017). The drawback is that a person may get demotivated when there is no incentive to complete the activity. Extrinsic motivation can be shown in someone who chooses to work at a job they detest because of the income and benefits.

Behavior can reveal a person's needs, goals, and desires. How driven a person is to achieve goals may be shown in their actions. One may tell if someone is driven to advance or gain a raise, for instance, by observing someone who has a hardworking demeanor. How driven a person is demonstrated by their actions (Plouffe, 2017). Stimuli are the forces that either push or pull a person mostly in the direction of such a motivating element. Stimuli induce behavior. A person is propelled into action as a result of becoming mentally or physiologically motivated. An individual becomes drawn into action as a result of environmental motivation. An individual's motivation can be inferred from their behavior. For instance, a person who imitates others does so out of wanting to fit in with the group (Mitchell & James, 2019). A person who is the life of the party is another illustration; they are driven to be the focus of attention.

Some sources of inspiration and motivation include:

Social media: Social media can be a great source of inspiration and motivation. Social media inspires and motivates people to connect with others with similar interests and goals (Humphrey et al., 2019). People can share ideas, advice, and support with others pursuing similar objectives through social media. Social media can also provide a sense of community and belonging for people who might otherwise feel isolated.

Books: Books can be a great source of inspiration and motivation. By reading about someone else's journey, people can be reminded of the possibilities for an individual's life. Additionally, books can provide us with new ideas and perspectives, which can help us to stay motivated and inspired (Maslow, 2019). Books can be a great source of inspiration and motivation. They can provide us with new ideas, help people see things in a different light, and give us the courage to pursue our dreams. However, it is important to remember that not all books are created equal. Some books are better than others at providing the motivation and inspiration needed to succeed. When choosing a book to read for inspiration and motivation, select one that is well-written and engaging (Locke & Latham, 2019). Additionally, look for a book that is relevant to your situation and provides practical advice that you can use to achieve your goals.

Movies: Movies can be a great source of inspiration and motivation. Watching someone else pursue their dreams can remind people of their dreams and goals (Bonifacio, 2017). Additionally, movies can provide people with a sense of hope and possibility, which can help us to stay motivated and inspired. They can also give people new ideas, help them see things from different perspectives, and remind them of what's important in life. There are all sorts of movies out there that can help us achieve people's goals, and it's up to them to find the ones that speak to us the most.

Music: Music can be a great source of inspiration and motivation. By listening to music we enjoy, people can remind individuals of the things we are passionate about. Additionally, music can help to boost people's mood and energy levels, which can help people to stay motivated and inspired (Bonifacio, 2017). Music is often cited as a source of inspiration and motivation. It can provide a boost when one needs it most and help one tap into their creative side. While there's no one-size-fits-all approach, certain genres or specific tracks may be more effective for some people than others. Furthermore, being in nature can provide a sense of peace and calm that can be helpful in finding inspiration and motivation. Sometimes it can be helpful to take a break from the hustle and bustle of the world and just appreciate the beauty around. One way is that nature can provide a sense of peace and tranquility, which can be helpful in reducing stress and anxiety levels (Plouffe, 2017). Additionally, spending time in nature can help to boost mood and increase energy levels, both of which can be helpful in terms of finding inspiration and motivation (Maslow, 2019). Additionally, being in nature can help to stimulate the senses and the mind, which can also be helpful in terms of finding inspiration and motivation.

Exercise is a great way to release endorphins, which can help improve your mood and give you motivation. Setting small goals for yourself and celebrating each accomplishment to keep yourself moving forward can be helpful. It can help clear people's minds, give one a sense of accomplishment, and provide a release from stress (Bird & Mendenhall, 2017). Exercise can also give you more energy and help you sleep better, leading to improved focus and concentration. On the other hand, spending time with supportive people can be a great way to find motivation. It can be helpful to have people who believe in themselves and their ability to achieve great things. Therefore, spending time with positive people can be motivating and inspiring (Plouffe, 2017). Being around supportive and encouraging people can help you feel more confident and motivated to pursue your goals. Additionally, if you ever feel stuck or lost, talking to someone supportive can help you get back on track.

Helping others can also be a great source of motivation. It can feel good to know that you are making a difference in someone else's life and doing something to improve the world. There are many ways to help others, and each person has unique talents and abilities that they can share (Plouffe, 2017). When we help others, we not only make their lives better, but we also make our own lives better. Helping others can give us a sense of purpose and satisfaction and inspire us to do more and be more. On the other side, creating a vision board of one's dreams can be a great way to find inspiration and motivation. It can be helpful to see your dreams and goals written down or illustrated in front of you to remind you of what you are working towards. By looking at one's dreams and goals, one can better understand what one wants to achieve and how you can achieve it.

Additionally, a **vision board** can help to keep you focused on your goals, remind you of your progress, and give you a visual representation of your dreams (Bird & Mendenhall, 2017). Furthermore, taking a break and doing something fun can also be helpful in finding motivation. It is important to remember to take time for yourself and do things that make you happy. Finding a mentor or coach can be a great way to get motivated. It can be helpful to have someone experienced and knowledgeable to guide you and give you advice.

Ways of Finding inspiration and motivation

Give oneself positive affirmations: A positive affirmation is a statement that affirms, declares, or affirms something about oneself. It is a way of planting a positive seed in your mind that will grow and blossom over time (Maslow, 2019). Some people find inspiration and motivation by giving themselves positive affirmations. By repeating positive statements to themselves, some people find that they are able to increase their confidence and self-esteem, which can lead to increased motivation. Additionally, some people find that writing down their positive affirmations and reading them back to themselves regularly can help keep them focused and motivated.

Practice gratitude: Gratitude is the quality of being thankful and appreciative. It is a way of looking at the world and seeing the good in people and situations. When one is grateful, one is happier and more positive. Practicing gratitude helps find inspiration and motivation because it allows individuals to focus on the positive aspects of their life. When people focus on the positive, they are more likely to be inspired and motivated to achieve their goals. Additionally, gratitude can help people see the good in others, which can inspire them to be kind and helpful.

Take care of one's physical well-being: Your physical well-being is important to your overall health and well-being. Eating healthy, exercising, and getting enough sleep are all ways to take care of your physical well-being (Bird & Mendenhall, 2017). Different people find different things helpful in terms of finding inspiration and motivation. However, taking care of one's physical well-being can be beneficial in this regard, as it can help promote a sense of overall physical and mental well-being. Additionally, maintaining a healthy lifestyle can help provide the energy and motivation needed to pursue one's goals.

Simplifying one's life: Simplifying your life means getting rid of the unnecessary things that clutter your life and make it more difficult. It is a way of decluttering one's life so that one can focus on what is truly important (Bird & Mendenhall, 2017). There are a number of ways that simplifying one's life can help to find inspiration and motivation. One way is that it can help to clear away distractions and allow more time for reflection and intro-spection. This can lead to a greater understanding of oneself and what one wants to achieve.

Additionally, simplifying can help to reduce stress levels, which can, in turn, improve focus and concentration. This can be bene-ficial when trying to find inspiration for new projects or goals. Finally, simplifying can also promote a sense of contentment and satisfaction, which can be motivating.

Learning: Learning something new is a great way to keep your mind active and engaged. Learning something new can help in finding motivation and inspiration in several ways. First, it can provide a sense of accomplishment and pride that can motivate (Argyris, 2019). Second, it can give you a new perspective on things and help you see things in a different light, which can be inspiring. Third, it can help you meet new people and make new friends, which can also be motivating and inspiring.

Beings present in the moment: Being present at the moment means being fully aware of what is happening around you and in your own life. It is a way of living in the present moment and not letting your mind wander into the past or future. There are a few ways that being present in the moment can help in finding motivation and inspiration (Amernic, & Craig, 2019). One way is that when one is present in the moment, one is more likely to be aware of their surroundings and the things happening around them. This can help individuals find things that inspire them and motivate them. Another way is that being present in the moment can help one to focus on the task at hand and not be distracted by other things (McClelland, 2019). This can help one to be more motivated to complete the task and to do it well.

Connect with your higher power or spirituality: Connecting with a higher power or one's spirituality can give you peace and calm. Everyone's experience with their higher power or spirituality is unique (Bird & Mendenhall, 2017). However, many people find that connecting with their higher power or spirituality can help them find motivation and inspiration. For some, this may mean attending religious services or participating in spiritual practices such as meditation or prayer (Maslow, 2019). Others may find inspiration and motivation through nature, art, or music. Whatever the source of inspiration, connecting with your higher power or spirituality can help you find the motivation and inspiration you need to pursue your goals.

Being mindful of one's thoughts and actions: Mindfulness is the quality of being aware and present. Mindful of their thoughts and actions allows them to be more aware of the present moment and find motivation and inspiration within themselves. It also allows them to be more aware of their thoughts and actions impact on others, which can be a source of motivation and inspiration.

Let go of perfectionism: Perfectionism is the quality of being perfect or flawless. It is often an unrealistic standard that we set for ourselves and others. Perfectionism can be a major barrier to finding motivation and inspiration. When we're focused on being perfect, we're often so worried about making mistakes that we don't allow ourselves to explore and experiment (Bird & Mendenhall, 2017). This can lead to stagnation and frustration, which can be very discouraging. Instead, try to focus on the process of creating and learning and be okay with making mistakes along the way. This will help one to stay motivated and inspired and ultimately help one to create better work.

Embrace your imperfections: Embracing one's imperfections means accepting oneself as one is. It recognizes that one is human and that one is not perfect. Imperfections can help people find motivation and inspiration because they remind them that they are human and that we all have different strengths and weaknesses

(Amernic & Craig, 2019). It's important to remember that we don't have to be perfect to be successful or to lead happy and fulfilling lives. Embracing their imperfections can help them feel more confident and motivated to pursue their goals.

In an ever-changing world, it can be difficult to find inspiration and motivation. However, there are a few things that one can do to help find these things. First, try to find something that one is passionate about. Once one has found something that is passionate about, it will be much easier to find the motivation to pursue it. Secondly, trying to surround oneself with positive people who will support one's dreams and goals. These people can help to inspire and motivate one to achieve one's goals. Finally, one should not be afraid to take risks. Sometimes, the best way to find inspiration and motivation is to take a leap of faith and pursue something that one is really interested in, even if it is outside of one's comfort zone.

References

Amernic, J., & Craig, R. (2019). Motivation, inspiration, and the public accounting profession. Issues in Accounting Education, 34(3), 559-576.

Argyris, C. (2019). On organizational learning. Malden, MA: Wiley-Blackwell.

Avolio, B. J., & Bass, B. M. (2019). Full-range leadership development: Manual for the multifactor leadership questionnaire. Thousand Oaks, CA: Sage.

Bird, S. M., & Mendenhall, M. E. (2017). Finding inspiration and motivation in an ever-changing world. Industrial and Organizational Psychology: Perspectives on Science and Practice, 10(3), 327-329.

Bonifacio, A. (2017). Finding inspiration and motivation in an ever-changing world. Management Research Review, 40(3), 314-325.

Carmeli, A., & Tishler, A. (2018). The relationship between top management teams' shared inspiration and firms' innovative outcomes. Journal of Business Venturing, 33(1), 21–36.

Chakravarthy, B., & Doeringer, P. (2019). The economics of motivation and learning. In J. E. Smith & M. D. Teachman (Eds.), Handbook of labor economics (Vol. 6A, pp. 495–543). Amsterdam, Netherlands: Elsevier.

Deci, E. L., & Ryan, R. M. (2019). Self-determination theory: Basic psychological needs in motivation, development, and wellness. New York, NY: Guilford Press.

Gagné, M., & Deci, E. L. (2017). Self-determination theory and work motivation. In K. D. Elsbach & R. H. Ashford (Eds.), Handbook of organizational psychology (Vol. 2, pp. 579-600).

Wiley Online Library.

Gelfand, M. J., & Raver, J. L. (2019). Culture, motivation, and team performance. Advances in Experimental Social Psychology, 56, 293-350.

Hepburn, C., & Simon, J. (2019). Emotion in organizations. Thousand Oaks, CA: Sage.

Humphrey, S. E., Nahrgang, J. D., & Morgeson, F. P. (2019). Integrating motivation, social, and contextual factors in leadership research: A meta-analytic review and test of a theoretical model. The Leadership Quarterly, 30(1), 192-217.

Kanfer, R., & Ackerman, P. L. (2019). Motivation theory and industrial and organizational psychology. In M. D. Dunnette & L. M. Hough (Eds.), Handbook of industrial and organizational psychology (Vol. 1, pp. 75-170). Palo Alto, CA: Consulting Psychologists Press.

Locke, E. A., & Latham, G. P. (2019). Goal setting: A framework for self-control. In E. A. Locke (Ed.), Goal setting: Theory, research, and application (pp. 21–33). Hillsdale, NJ: Erlbaum.

Maslow, A. H. (2019). A theory of human motivation. In C. R. Rogers (Ed.), Carl Rogers on personal power (pp. 25–38). New York, NY: Delacorte Press.

McClelland, D. C. (2019). The achievement motive. In D. C. McClelland (Ed.), Motives and personality (pp. 1–20). New York, NY: McGraw-Hill.

Mitchell, T. R., & James, L. R. (2019). Motivation: Directing behavior toward goals (5th ed.). Fort Worth, TX: Harcourt Brace.

Pinder, C. C. (2019). Work motivation in organizational behavior. Upper Saddle River, NJ: Prentice Hall.

Pink, D. H. (2017). Drive: The surprising truth about what motivates us. Riverhead Books.

Plouffe, C. R. (2017). Finding inspiration and motivation in an ever-changing world. International Journal of Environmental Research and Public Health, 14(3), 300.

Chapter 9:

Opinions on diagnosing mental health disorders

Written by: Tara Y. Chen

Introduction

Diagnosing mental health disorders is important for helping individuals understand their condition, symptoms, and how to receive proper treatment. The experience of receiving a mental health diagnosis can be very stressful and varies for each person. Although Canada has an excellent healthcare system, there are several aspects that can be improved, including the implementation of artificial intelligence. This chapter discusses Dr. Austin Mardon's opinions on the different aspects of diagnosing mental health disorders in Canada, and how families can support their loved ones with mental health conditions.

Receiving mental health disorder diagnoses

Primary care physicians diagnose a wide range of mental health disorders around the world. Despite modern research and an improved understanding of the brain, some disorders may be misdiagnosed or undiagnosed, which negatively impacts the patient's quality of life (Rogers et al., 2021). Globally, the prevalence of mental health disorders increases each year and most are not treated effectively. Additionally, there are over 46 million individuals with at least one major mental health disease, according to an analysis conducted by the National Institute of Health (Rogers et al., 2021).

For Dr. Austin Mardon, although his schizophrenia and post-traumatic stress disorder diagnoses were determined 31 years ago (as of November 2022), they were still conducted accurately. At the time of his diagnosis, Dr. Mardon had experienced lucid dreams, was talking to himself, and was hospitalised. In addition to being sick for several years, both his mother and great grandmother had been previously diagnosed with schizophrenia. Thus due to his genetics and symptoms, it was fairly easy for physicians to diagnose him. Typically, these kinds of diagnoses involve several months of tests, but the process only required one week for Dr. Mardon. Typically, after receiving a diagnosis, many patients struggle to receive proper treatment due to factors such as a lack of doctors, lack of government funding, and more (Rogers et al., 2021). These individuals tend to be at greater risk of attempting suicide, losing employment, and abuse. Treatment for hospitalised patients without insurance may even exceed $5000 United States dollar (USD) per week, which is a financial difficulty for many (Rogers et al., 2021).

For Dr. Mardon, he recalls screaming uncontrollably and feeling upset after receiving his diagnoses because he felt that his life and dreams were coming to an end. However, he soon realised that his life was not completely doomed and that he could make adjustments to improve it. Luckily for Dr. Mardon, the physicians kindly explained his symptoms to him, and he felt that his diagnosis was helpful.

The timing of Dr. Mardon's diagnosis was also beneficial to him. If he had received the diagnoses at an earlier point in his life, he felt that he would have abruptly stopped his career and become homeless. Luckily, due to the timing of his diagnosis, he was able to apply for grants for individuals with mental health disorders, which helped improve his career trajectory. Additionally, although medications for mental health disorders were not as effective 31 years ago as they are today, Dr. Mardon likes to quote a Chinese belief that encountering a crisis is an opportunity to improve one's life. Thus, despite feeling devastated about his diagnoses, Dr. Mardon found positivity in his situation.

How Canada can improve the accuracy of mental health diagnoses

In Canada, 20% of individuals suffer from mental health disorders, and will need access to proper treatment and accurate diagnoses (Follwell et al., 2021). It is also likely that the number of individuals with mental health disorders will increase in the near future due to the stress and anxiety associated with the coronavirus disease 2019 (COVID-19) pandemic, which warrants an even greater need for mental health support (Follwell et al., 2021).

In Canada, diagnosis and treatment are delivered by psychiatrists, psychologists, family doctors, social workers and more (Follwell et al., 2021). Luckily, Canada provides free healthcare via provincial and territorial healthcare plans, and patients may receive health benefits from their employer. However, coverage still varies between provinces and territories, and patients may need to pay for some health services out of pocket (Follwell et al., 2021). Specifically, only family doctors and psychiatrists are covered by government healthcare plans. Healthcare support from nurses, psychologists, and social workers need to be paid by the patient or from health benefits from a job (Bartram, 2019).

It is estimated that two-thirds of Canadians have access to employer health benefits. For the remaining one-third who do not have company benefits, it is unlikely that they pay for necessary healthcare services out of pocket (Bartram, 2019). Unfortunately, this decreases the amount of support, treatment, and accurate diagnoses for individuals of a lower socioeconomic status. These issues started in the 1950s and 1960s in Canada, when the coverage policies were first established (Bartram, 2019). Compared to the United Kingdom where the government spends 13% of funds on public healthcare, Canada only spends between 5% to 7% of taxpayers' money on health (Bartram, 2019). This allocation of taxpayer money in Canada has detrimental effects on whether youth and young adults can receive proper mental health diagnoses and treatments. It is estimated that 12% of Canadians over the age of 15 require mental health check-ups, but only two-thirds receive proper help (Bartram, 2019).

According to Dr. Mardon, there aren't enough doctors in Canada to diagnose and treat everyone who has a mental health disorder. There are different severity levels to mental health, and individuals with more mild forms may not necessarily benefit from seeing a doctor or psychiatrist. For instance, Dr. Mardon mentions that individuals with minor forms of anxiety and non-clinical depression who see psychiatrists put a strain on the Canadian healthcare system. This is because individuals with severe mental health diagnoses will have less access to psychiatrists due to the limited supply. He believes that the Canadian healthcare system should prioritise diagnosing and treating individuals who are the most ill. Helping them receive support earlier in their illness progression will prevent homelessness, jail time, and other problems that may impact the individual's quality of life. Overall, by intervening earlier for persons with severe mental health disorders, Canada can decrease the financial burden of treating mental health.

Moreover, the stigma associated with mental health disorders may prevent individuals from seeking help earlier (Follwell et al., 2021). Patients may also be at risk of committing suicide or abusing substances due to discrimination, which further decreases their likelihood of receiving a proper diagnosis and treatment (Follwell et al., 2021). Fortunately, there are a few organisations in Canada that strive to improve mental healthcare diagnosis. For instance, the Mental Health Commission of Canada and HealthCareCAN have gathered over 30 leaders from Canadian healthcare organisations to try to place a greater emphasis on caring for mental health in the workplace (Follwell et al., 2021). They have focused on addressing mental health stigmas at workplaces, and encouraging healthcare professionals to have recovery-oriented appointments (Follwell et al., 2021).

Dr. Mardon views and understands that mental health disorders are artificial constructs, and are not necessarily biological in nature. Mental health disorders may also be more subjective or culturally relevant for some healthcare professionals. Dr. Mardon believes that it would be beneficial for the Canadian healthcare system if all healthcare providers could be aware of Canadian culture and perspectives on mental health. Foreign doctors who have immigrated to and practise in Canada may impact whether mental health disorders are accurately diagnosed because they grew up with different cultural and religious beliefs. Additionally, foreign doctors may take religious offence or may not be familiar with Canadian slang, which negatively impacts their ability to relate to their patients and provide accurate diagnoses. Some cultures are also not as open minded as Canadian culture, and mental health may be a social stigma in foreign countries. Dr. Mardon believes it is preferable to have more Canadian-trained doctors, nurses, and healthcare providers who understand the importance of mental health. Unfortunately, with the recent news that the Canadian government plans to increase the number of doctors in Canada by having foreign doctors, Dr. Mardon believes that mental health diagnoses will only continue to worsen in the near future.

Overall, Dr. Mardon believes that mental health disorder diagnoses can be improved by having mostly Canadian doctors, and by focusing on individuals who are the most ill. Only then can Canada be relieved of its financial burden, and help the greatest number of individuals possible.

Artificial intelligence for diagnosing mental health disorders

The process of diagnosing mental health disorders is complicated due to subjective factors such as a diverse clinical presentation amongst individuals, the specific stage of the disorder, the difference in educational knowledge between physicians of different countries, subjective summary of symptoms experienced by the patient, subjective observations made by family members, and more (Abd-alrazaq et al., 2022). Objective methods of diagnosing mental health disorders are not widely available, which may allow for accidental misdiagnoses. Moreover, determining a diagnosis is time-consuming and requires a substantial amount of resources (Abd-alrazaq et al., 2022).

Fortunately, modern technology has led to the development of artificial intelligence (AI), which may be applied to aid healthcare teams around the world. AI is developed by teaching machines a set of complex rules or patterns, which enable them to arrive at conclusions in a more objective and rapid manner (Abd-alrazaq et al., 2022). This can be especially useful for providing physicians with a second medical opinion, and establishing a universal standard when diagnosing and treating patients (Abd-alrazaq et al., 2022). For example, social bots have been developed to help dementia patients feel less lonely, and navigate their daily medical needs. Virtual psychotherapists have also been developed to expand the number of mental health treatments that can be provided, and deal with an inadequate amount of healthcare workers (Abd-alrazaq et al., 2022). Recently, AI has been used to assess patterns in patients' genes, behaviours, and environment to detect certain mental disorders such as schizophrenia, post-traumatic stress disorder, and bipolar disorder. The effectiveness of AI in mental health is currently being assessed by researchers (Abd-alrazaq et al., 2022).

For instance, in a review of over 30 studies assessing the effectiveness of AI in diagnosing schizophrenia, the results were greatly varied. Accuracy of the algorithm ranged from 61% to 99.3% and specificity ranged from 40.9% to 98.6% (Abd-alrazaq et al., 2022). Other studies also observed the accuracy of AI for diagnosing post-traumatic stress disorder. The accuracy for these algorithms were slightly better than that of schizophrenia, and ranged from 89.2% to 92.3% (Abd-alrazaq et al., 2022). Other mental health disorders diagnosed with AI also showed similar results. The diagnosis accuracy was between 55%-100% for bipolar disorder, between 45%-97% for autism spectrum disorder, and between 66%-100% for obsessive-compulsive disorder (Abd-alrazaq et al., 2022). Overall, results for accuracy varied greatly between different AI algorithms for different disorders. Fortunately, researchers have witnessed more accurate results when training AI using neuroimaging data rather than with genetic data. Moreover, they discovered that using solely genetic data, without the implementation of other factors such as environmental factors, led to lower accuracy rates (Abd-alrazaq et al., 2022). Thus, recent research in this field has been more focused on incorporating several factors into training AI algorithms.

Dr. Mardon believes that the use of artificial intelligence may be a solution to Canada's mental healthcare problems, such as a lack of doctors and funding. For instance, artificial intelligence can provide diagnoses for a greater number of individuals, and standardise the symptoms that indicate a specific diagnosis. Individuals will also not need to wait months to see a physician for a diagnosis. Instead, artificial intelligence provides a convenient and fast method of receiving information. However, Dr. Mardon believes that the current mental health apps that are based on artificial intelligence are not effective enough for diagnoses at the moment. However, he is on a committee for tech-based mental health solutions and is working towards receiving app approval.

Furthermore, while the use of artificial intelligence used in healthcare systems may be a relatively new concept, Dr. Mardon references a study from Science that reveals that artificial intelligence has a 75% chance of providing accurate diagnoses. Surprisingly, this is the same accuracy rate as most doctors. He believes that within the next few years, the accuracy of diagnoses from artificial intelligence will surpass that of doctors. There needs to be a few more clinical tests and studies before this technology can be widely implemented into healthcare systems. Dr. Mardon predicts that artificial intelligence will not necessarily replace doctors, but it will work alongside them to help diagnose mental health disorders more accurately.

Overall, as AI is being further tested and developed, it is likely to be implemented in healthcare systems in the near future. Dr. Mardon is hopeful that technology can support mental healthcare in Canada by providing quicker and more affordable diagnoses.

Aspects of mental health diagnosis that require more attention in Canada

Although mental health is a widely discussed topic in Canada, there are many aspects to its diagnosis and treatment. Policy makers decide where resources are allocated in treatment facilities, which impacts the type of care that patients receive. This may mean that some aspects of mental healthcare are set aside to provide more attention to other aspects.

Dr. Mardon believes that bipolar disorder, schizophrenia, and severe post-traumatic stress disorder are mental health crises that require more attention in Canada. He states that the majority of the homeless in Canada are individuals with schizophrenia or post-traumatic stress disorder, and that treating these patients can reduce the prevalence of homelessness. Healthcare services should also focus more on individuals who are in serious need of help because there is a limit to the amount of resources available. For the majority of individuals who are worried and anxious about their mental health, their symptoms can usually be treated with prescription medication.

Moreover, Dr. Mardon believes that prevention is another important aspect of mental health that requires more attention. This results in less money for physicians, more money for nurses, and more money required from taxpayers, which may result in more unhappy individuals. However, it is important to establish better addiction treatment and mental health programs, which can be financially beneficial in the long-run. This will require a greater need for social workers and psychiatric nurses to provide these services since physicians may not have the availability to talk to patients for extended periods of time.

Additionally, Dr. Mardon believes that Canadian healthcare systems should provide more aid to individuals suffering from social problems and financial problems, which often compound with mental illness. He believes that diagnosis by itself is not useful unless patients can afford their daily prescribed medications. He also supports public care and hospitalizations that are affordable, which can help a greater number of patients receive the treatment that they require. He believes that private healthcare systems would not be beneficial to Canada because patients with schizophrenia or other mental health disorders will be forgotten and untreated due to the high costs of treatment. Instead, patients who are overly worried with non-severe forms of mental illness will receive all the healthcare resources, leaving none for others.

Overall, a focus on prevention, building better treatment centres, and funding public healthcare are areas that Dr. Mardon believes Canada should focus on.

How family and friends can support individuals with mental health disorders

Receiving a mental health diagnosis can be stressful for both the patient and family. Fortunately, there are many methods and resources that can help both parties navigate the situation. Family and friends can be an incredibly valuable support system who can help the patient during their treatment and recovery progress.

According to the American Psychological Association, family members and friends may help encourage the patient to participate in therapy sessions and be more open to healthcare providers (American Psychological Association [APA], 2019). Educating themselves on the mental health disorder can also help loved ones learn what to expect and how to provide effective emotional support for the patient (APA, 2019). Loved ones may also help ease the patient's anxiety by accompanying them to health appointments and support groups (APA, 2019).

Dr. Mardon believes that family and friends can support individuals who recently received a mental health diagnosis by talking to the physician and social worker, reading appropriate books on how to deal with situations, and educating themselves on the disorder. This may ease the stress or confusion, and teach them ways to be supportive and helpful to their loved one. Additionally, he suggests that speaking with the individual with the mental health diagnosis is an efficient method of learning more about the disorder and understanding them better. It is also important to support the individual and participate in their dreams.

In addition, the Canadian Mental Health Association provides a list of resources that caregivers, family, and friends may use to support their loved one. The Schizophrenia Society offers help and local support groups for family members with a loved one impacted by the condition. The NAMI Family-to-Family Education Program also educates families impacted by severe mental health by providing a free 2-month course on how to navigate the situation. Moreover, Parents for Children's Mental Health provides support for youth and their families by connecting them with local communities who can provide resources.

Overall, family and friends are integral to helping their loved one progress well during their mental health treatment. By educating themselves and seeking help from resources, family and friends can provide the support and love that mental health patients need.

Conclusion

In conclusion, the process of receiving a mental health diagnosis differs for everyone and can be a stressful experience. Although Canada's healthcare system is well established, its mental health services can be improved in several ways. Dr. Mardon believes that focusing on patients with severe illness, and improving public facilities and addiction centres can decrease homelessness and the number of individuals suffering from mental disorders. In the future, Dr. Mardon also predicts that AI will have a great amount of influence on how mental health disorders are diagnosed and treated. Overall, in addition to improving the healthcare system, having family and friends who are supportive can greatly improve a patient's mood and treatment progress.

References

Abd-alrazaq, A., Alhuwail, D., Schneider, J., Toro, C. T., Ahmed, A., Alzubaidi, M., Alajlani, M. &

Househ, M. (2022). The performance of artificial intelligence-driven technologies in diagnosing mental health disorders: an umbrella review. *NPJ digital medicine*, 5(1), 87. https://doi.org/10.1038/s41746-022-00631-8

American Psychological Association. (2019). *Supporting a family member with serious*

mental illness. American Psychological Association. https://www.apa.org/topics/mental-health/support-serious-mental-illness

Bartram, M. (2019). Income-based inequities in access to mental health services in Canada. *Can*

J Public Health, 110(4), 395-403. https://doi.org/10.17269/s41997-019-00204-5

Follwell, J. E., Chunduri, S., Samuelson-Kiraly, C., Watters, N., & Mitchell, J. I. (2021). The Quality

Mental Health Care Network: A roadmap to improving quality mental healthcare in Canada. *Healthc Manage Forum*, 34(2), 100-106. https://doi.org/10.1177/0840470420974713

Rogers, R., Hartigan, S. E., & Sanders, C. E. (2021). Identifying Mental Disorders in Primary Care:

Diagnostic Accuracy of the Connected Mind Fast Check (CMFC) Electronic Screen. *J Clin Psychol Med Settings*, 28(4), 882-896. https://doi.org/10.1007/s10880-021-09820-1

Chapter 10:

Perspectives and misconceptions on seeking mental health treatment in today's society

Written by: Michael Phan

Even when absolutely necessary, some individuals are reluctant to ask for help when they need it. Consider a student in a vast lecture hall holding over five hundred other students. If there ever arose a concept that the professor didn't explain as clearly, students may find the act of raising their hand and asking for further clarification extremely daunting. This can oftentimes be the result of the student's own belief that, by seeking help, others will judge their academic capabilities and prowess (Ryan et al., 1998). It is this very misconception – that asking for help means that you are incompetent – that is just one of the many barriers which make it incredibly difficult for those suffering from mental illnesses to seek the support systems they need to maintain some semblance of a normal life.

This is especially plain to see when it comes to seeking mental health treatment. Even in today's society, there are many destructive and unproductive perspectives and misconceptions regarding this topic that can deter those from seeking help when they need it the most. In this chapter, Dr. Austin Mardon provides his unique experiences and outlook when it comes to these misconceptions and how they altered his life before and after his diagnosis.

In the grand scheme of things, stigma is a major player in various opinions regarding severe mental illness. Stigma can be divided into three categories: self, public, and institutionalised (Pattyn et al., 2014). Self stigma is how you view yourself which, Dr. Austin Mardon says, can be the worst of the three categories – as it has the ability to eat you up from the inside and holds the most power. In reference to the aforementioned connection between seeking help and self-portrayed competency, individuals may find it shameful to seek help because of this personal stigma. While it is important to have some degree of self-reliance and independence, humans are social beings that depend on their community for support. There have been numerous studies that have shown that people who have a support system and are able to rely on others exhibit a higher degree of communication skills, which ultimately decreases the prevalence of mental health issues such as depression and anxiety (Fasihi Harandi et al., 2017).

Public stigma is how others, such as friends, family, or even strangers view you. In Dr. Mardon's case, he recalls when – after disclosing his mental illness to his extended family – his aunt urged him to get sterilised to prevent him from passing on his genetic mental disorder. The many misconceptions of mental illness feed into this stigma and eventually produce damaging stereotypes and prejudice. Sadly, perception is reality – meaning those who have baseless assumptions regarding mental illness will treat the afflicted much differently, thus robbing them of the same opportunities anybody else would expect. Based on a recent review, it was observed that one of the most shared desires among those suffering from mental illness to improve their overall quality of life was to feel a certain sense of belonging (Connell et al., 2012). Naturally, this sense can ultimately be achieved by having meaningful relationships with others and while not having to worry about stigma – but it is not so simple for those with these severe conditions. To even open up about one's diagnosis can be very daunting, especially with mental disorders that are not commonly known and have a significant level of stigma surrounding it. This is likely because of the fear that friends or family will treat them differently. Besides the blatant discrimination and disrespect of mental illness, it is not uncommon for some people to simply deny its existence and dismiss any effects that it may have on the afflicted (DE HERT et al., 2011). By downplaying their illness, this shows that one would be unable to confide in them for any kind of emotional support. The fear of being not understood alone is likely enough to deter someone with severe mental disorders from opening up to others.

A cross analysis of two independent surveys comprising around two thousand participants found that there are three primary stereotypes regarding mental illness. For one, many believe that those with severe mental illness should be isolated from society because of their perceived unpredictable nature. Dr. Mardon himself has personally witnessed this particular sentiment first hand, as he finds that many people believe that those suffering from severe mental illness are but "...one step away from being a criminal." This misconception, that those with mental illnesses are psychologically volatile and a danger to society, represents the opinions that a significant portion of the population stands by. In the public eye, these generalisations can eventually evolve into fear. This fear can in turn motivate these individuals to either dissociate themselves away from those suffering from mental illnesses or call for the forceful isolation of the latter from society altogether (Angermeyer & Dietrich, 2006). Dr. Austin Mardon saw this firsthand when he had initially opened up about his diagnosis of schizophrenia to those around him. While he was expecting unconditional support from those he held dear, many people – such as his parents-in-law – ended up ostracising him from their lives. Even to this day, there are friends that Dr. Mardon has not seen in decades. What is most unfortunate about this is that ostracization can actually perpetuate mental illness and make things more difficult (Wesselmann et al., 2018). This is due to the fact that, without a proper support system, it can be very hard to cope and restabilize one's life back to normalcy.

Next, many believe that those with severe mental illness should not be trusted with their own autonomy because of their lack of responsibility (more on this later). Finally, similar to the previous stereotype, many believe that those with mental illness must be watched over as if they were children (Corrigan & Watson, 2002). Autonomy can mean a lot for those with severe mental illnesses, as it allows them to feel as though they still exhibit some control over the diagnosis that changed their life for good. In reference to the example about how students associate needing help with a lack of competence, this is very similar to how those with mental illnesses feel. This sense of autonomy is not limited to interpersonal interactions, but it can also extend to intrapersonal interactions – how they interact with themselves– as well. In mental illnesses that are known to be more volatile such as BPD (bipolar disorder) or schizophrenia, it can be very difficult to make rational decisions all of the time. It is said that to truly be autonomous, one must be doing certain things that their mind can justify or rationalise if they were given time to reflect on it. To act on desires that, if they were given time to reflect, are not representative of what they would actually do would decrease the autonomy they have over their person. Yes, many of us who do not have mental illnesses can definitely recall a time that we made a spur of the moment decision that was not fully thought out. There may be times where one may spontaneously decide to get a tattoo without really considering the consequences of their actions and simply letting the adrenaline handle it from there, as an example. The main difference here is that those with mental illnesses, even if they have lashed out fifty times prior, do not have the benefit of learning from their mistakes. They will feel obligated, compelled even, to do what their mental illness forces them to do and continue this behavioural pattern (Bergamin et al., 2022). Considering the psychosis that is often associated as a symptom of schizophrenia, the confusion and disorientation that ensues can most likely compromise one's sense of autonomy.

It is important to note that stereotypes do not necessarily need to be inherently true or false. Indeed, there are certain stereotypes that are quite necessary and applicable in life. For instance, if you are walking late at night and are considering taking a route that cuts through a sketchy area, you will likely remember the stereotype that most dark, run-down areas are dangerous. It is then up to your own judgement to decide whether you want to take that risk or not. However, stereotypes are oversimplified caricatures that can often be damaging to the person, place, or thing that is being referenced. While it is statistically true that those with mental illness can be more likely to exhibit more violent behaviour, it is not fair or just to automatically assume that anybody with mental illness will unpredictably lash out (Cho et al., 2019). If the relatively higher proportion of violent individuals with mental illness was enough to constitute generalising every single individual with that condition, then it would be hypocritical to not do the same for men as a whole – who commit around eighty percent of all global homicides (United Nations, 2019).

Furthermore, these generalisations may actually dehumanise those with mental illness. Instead of describing an individual as "somebody who is suffering from schizophrenia", these stereotypes would characterise that individual as "a schizophrenic" – which labels them based on their affliction, rather than their holistic self (Corrigan & Watson, 2002). As Boysen et al (2019) put it, dehumanisation can be described as the refusal to accept an individual as a functional member of society – which can often go as far as treating the "dehumanised" as animals and savages. This is by no means a new occurrence. As much as many would wish to forget – or even, attempt to erase–, humanity over the years has consistently developed a bad habit of discriminating against those that are different, those that deviate from the norm, whether that be spiritually, physically, or in this case – mentally. The Holocaust, for instance, was fueled by the Nazi ideology that Jewish people were "pests." Slavery was fueled by the idea that black people were "apes"(Boysen et al., 2019). This dehumanisation of those that suffer from mental illness, as Dr. Mardon puts it, portrays them as nothing but potential criminals. The complexity of a human being's life, with years of developing skills, learning new things, enjoying art and food, and building relationships strictly reduced to an illness that they did not choose to have. Even when they have never committed a crime in their life, the way that society paints them practically gives them a life sentence.

The idea that mental illnesses should not be taken as seriously as physical, more tangible illnesses such as cancer or diabetes is another problematic misconception. In doing so, the blame is pinned on the afflicted individual, who is made to believe that their condition is "all in their head". While this has been proven to not be the case, there are many who claim that mental illness simply does not exist (Benning, 2016). As it turns out, the fact that severe mental disorders can consequently result in physical illness is definitive proof of its existence. For instance, there have been various studies conducted in North America that link obesity to people with schizophrenia with a prevalence of 60%. While this link can be related to common factors such as inactivity and a calorie-dense diet, there are certain factors that are directly related to schizophrenia such as depressive symptoms that can lead to increased prevalence of obesity (De Hert et al., 2011).

This public stigma is taken a step further when considering the systemic repercussions of these misconceptions, thus perpetuating institutionalised stigma. This systemic attitude towards mental illness and those suffering from it may ultimately impact their accessibility to certain necessities. Recall the second stereotype that portrayed those with severe mental illness as irresponsible. With this crude generalisation of those with mental illness, employers may reconsider hiring an otherwise qualified candidate solely because of their condition. In a British survey, it was found that around forty percent of those suffering from mental health problems say that they were rejected from a job because they had disclosed their condition to the hiring manager. Furthermore, it was discovered that employers reportedly preferred hiring those with physical disabilities over those with mental disorders (Wheat et al., 2010). This then begs the question: Should one hide their condition in the event that it reflects poorly on their application, or should they be honest? This dilemma does not just stop at employment, however, as even landlords are likely to discriminate against potential tenants due to their mental disabilities (Hammel et al., 2017).

So what does this mean for those suffering from mental illness? It means that this institutionalised stigma makes it tremendously harder for them to reintegrate into society and attempt to win back the normalcy in their life. Owing to this, Dr. Mardon firmly believes that he was fortunate enough to be diagnosed at a point in his career where he had many options available. Despite his diagnosis, he was able to persist and apply for grants which allowed him to pursue his PhD in geography from Greenwich University. Sadly, there is not always such a positive outcome for those with mental disorders, with some studies suggesting that twenty to fourty percent of the homeless population suffer from some kind of mental illness (Treatment Advocacy Center, 2016). Whether mental illness leads to poverty, or poverty leads to mental illness seems to be paradoxical in nature, as studies show that there are in fact environmental risk factors that can increase the likelihood of mental illness (Burns et al., 2013).

With that said, it is clear to see why it is so difficult to reach out for help in a world that seems to demonise those suffering from severe mental illness. In order to allow those who need help to seek it, the narrative surrounding mental illness must be reestablished on a personal and systemic level. One such strategy to address this stigma is to urge the media to stop showcasing erroneous depictions of mental illness and to urge the public to not buy into the negative stereotypes of mental illness. Although it is important for the media to remain impartial and report every segment, they must be made aware of the power that their words have on the public's perception of others. Considering the media coverage of vaccinations, many studies have shown that the spreading of misinformation has led to increased anxiety, depression, and panic, while also decreasing the public's trust in the credibility of many health professionals as well as the federal and regional governing body (Rocha et al., 2021). Education programs – that have been widely proven to be effective – should also be established, as research has shown that those with a higher knowledge of mental illness are much less likely to promote inaccurate stereotypes (Corrigan & Watson, 2002).

Failure to maintain proper mental health awareness and education can perpetuate fear, leading to the aforementioned stigma that can cyclize through generations. In Dr. Mardon's case, he had already gained insight and experience with severe mental illness by growing up with a mother and grandmother who were both diagnosed with schizophrenia. However, because individuals with severe mental illness remain a minority – with only 0.32% of the global population suffering from schizophrenia – many people do not fully understand how to interact with those with mental health conditions (World Health Organization, 2022).

One may believe that growing up in a household that is mentally and psychologically healthy would be extremely nourishing and beneficial, but Dr. Mardon believes that this is not always the case. He explains that, in a family of well-rounded star athletes, A+ students, and musical prodigies – i.e, the "perfect family" – things can go south very quickly as a result of a sudden diagnosis. This is because the family and friends (the support system) would not be well equipped with sufficient attitudes or coping mechanisms to handle the situation. This suffering is two-fold, as the afflicted individual has to deal with the everyday struggles of mental illness, while also grieving the dreams that they believe will never come into fruition (which does not always have to be true). In his own life, Dr. Mardon's father and – to a lesser extent – his sister understood the obligations that would come with having a loved one suffer from a severe mental illness. Dr. Mardon takes this a step further and explains that experience with severe mental illness in others can be beneficial even to those who were recently diagnosed, since it prepares them for what to expect.

Dr. Austin Mardon asserts that, while fear causes the most disconnect when it comes to mental health, human connection has the unique potential to counteract this fear. Indeed, one's perspective about mental illness is ultimately defined by their own personal experiences, which is the culmination of their upbringing, the media that they consume, as well as interactions with those with mental illnesses (Corrigan et al., 2004). Research has proven that discrimination is significantly reduced when the general public is able to regularly interact with those suffering from mental illness – especially those who are involved in their community and work hard to benefit society. These interactions seem to disprove their negative outlooks and show them that they are more than just their mental illness (Corrigan et al., 2004).

Ultimately, it is clear to see that society has a long way to go before mental illness is treated with the same decency and understanding that other, more physical and tangible, illnesses elicit. Dr. Austin Mardon's life has so far been nothing short of inspirational – as it shows that it is still possible to make the best out of a bad situation and persevere despite having your life flipped with a major diagnosis. The main barrier to a more inclusive society has to do with the public's preconceived notions and opinions surrounding those who are suffering from mental illnesses. From what was discussed earlier, it is important to recognize that these stereotypes can be very damaging, which is made worse by perpetuating them through future generations. To remedy this, educational programs, increased mindfulness by the media and increased contact with those living with these severe mental illnesses are needed, such that individuals are able to form their own opinions without the input from damaging and misleading sources.

References

Angermeyer, M. C., & Dietrich, S. (2006). Public beliefs about and attitudes towards people with mental illness: a review of population studies. Acta Psychiatrica Scandinavica, 113(3), 163–179. https://doi.org/10.1111/j.1600-0447.2005.00699.x

Benning, T. B. (2016). No such thing as mental illness? Critical reflections on the major ideas and legacy of Thomas Szasz. BJPsych Bulletin, 40(6), 292–295. https://doi.org/10.1192/pb.bp.115.053249

Bergamin, J., Luigjes, J., Kiverstein, J., Bockting, C. L., & Denys, D. (2022). Defining Autonomy in Psychiatry. Frontiers in Psychiatry, 13. https://doi.org/10.3389/fpsyt.2022.801415

Boysen, G. A., Isaacs, R. A., Tretter, L., & Markowski, S. (2019). Evidence for blatant dehumanization of mental illness and its relation to stigma. The Journal of Social Psychology, 160(3), 1–11. https://doi.org/10.1080/00224545.2019.1671301

Burns, J. K., Tomita, A., & Kapadia, A. S. (2013). Income inequality and schizophrenia: Increased schizophrenia incidence in countries with high levels of income inequality. International Journal of Social Psychiatry, 60(2), 185–196. https://doi.

org/10.1177/0020764013481426

Cho, W., Shin, W.-S., An, I., Bang, M., Cho, D.-Y., & Lee, S.-H. (2019). Biological Aspects of Aggression and Violence in Schizophrenia. Clinical Psychopharmacology and Neuroscience, 17(4), 475–486. https://doi.org/10.9758/cpn.2019.17.4.475

Clasen, M. (2017, October 24). How Evolution Designed Your Fear. Nautilus. https://nautil.us/how-evolution-designed-your-fear-236858/

Connell, J., Brazier, J., O'Cathain, A., Lloyd-Jones, M., & Paisley, S. (2012). Quality of life of people with mental health problems: a synthesis of qualitative research. Health and Quality of Life Outcomes, 10(1), 138. https://doi.org/10.1186/1477-7525-10-138

Corrigan, P. W., Markowitz, F. E., & Watson, A. C. (2004). Structural Levels of Mental Illness Stigma and Discrimination. Schizophrenia Bulletin, 30(3), 481–491. https://doi.org/10.1093/oxfordjournals.schbul.a007096

Corrigan, P. W., & Watson, A. C. (2002). Understanding the impact of stigma on people with mental illness. World Psychiatry : Official Journal of the World Psychiatric Association (WPA), 1(1), 16–20.

DE HERT, M., CORRELL, C. U., BOBES, J., CETKOVICH-BAKMAS, M., COHEN, D., ASAI, I., DETRAUX, J., GAUTAM, S., MÖLLER, H.-J., NDETEI, D. M., NEWCOMER, J. W., UWAKWE, R., & LEUCHT, S. (2011). Physical illness in patients with severe mental disorders. I. Prevalence, impact of medications and disparities in health care. World Psychiatry, 10(1), 52–77. https://doi.

org/10.1002/j.2051-5545.2011.tb00014.x

Fasihi Harandi, T., Mohammad Taghinasab, M., & Dehghan Nayeri, T. (2017). The correlation of social support with mental health: A meta-analysis. Electronic Physician, 9(9), 5212–5222. https://doi.org/10.19082/5212

Hammel, J., Smith, J., Scovill, S., Campbell, R., & Duan, R. (2017). RENTAL HOUSING DISCRIMINATION ON THE BASIS OF MENTAL DISABILITIES: RESULTS OF PILOT TESTING. U.S. Department of Housing and Urban Development Office of Policy Development and Research.

Morgan, A. J., Reavley, N. J., Jorm, A. F., & Beatson, R. (2017). Discrimination and support from friends and family members experienced by people with mental health problems: findings from an Australian national survey. Social Psychiatry and Psychiatric Epidemiology, 52(11), 1395–1403. https://doi.org/10.1007/s00127-017-1391-z

Pattyn, E., Verhaeghe, M., Sercu, C., & Bracke, P. (2014). Public stigma and self-stigma: differential association with attitudes toward formal and informal help seeking. Psychiatric Services (Washington, D.C.), 65(2), 232–238. https://doi.org/10.1176/appi.ps.201200561

Rocha, Y. M., de Moura, G. A., Desidério, G. A., de Oliveira, C. H., Lourenço, F. D., & de Figueiredo Nicolete, L. D. (2021). The impact of fake news on social media and its influence on health during the COVID-19 pandemic: a systematic review. Journal of Public Health. https://doi.org/10.1007/s10389-021-01658-z

Ryan, A. M., Gheen, M. H., & Midgley, C. (1998). Why do

some students avoid asking for help? An examination of the interplay among students' academic efficacy, teachers' social-emotional role, and the classroom goal structure. Journal of Educational Psychology, 90(3), 528–535. https://doi.org/10.1037/0022-0663.90.3.528

Treatment Advocacy Center. (2016). Serious Mental Illness and Homelessness. Office of Research & Public Affairs.

United Nations. (2019). Global study on homicide. Unodc.org. https://www.unodc.org/unodc/en/data-and-analysis/global-study-on-homicide.html

Wesselmann, E. D., Ispas, D., Olson, M. D., Swerdlik, M. E., & Caudle, N. M. (2018). Does perceived ostracism contribute to mental health concerns among veterans who have been deployed? PLOS ONE, 13(12), e0208438. https://doi.org/10.1371/journal.pone.0208438

Wheat, K., Brohan, E., Henderson, C., & Thornicroft, G. (2010). Mental illness and the workplace: conceal or reveal? Journal of the Royal Society of Medicine, 103(3), 83–86. https://doi.org/10.1258/jrsm.2009.090317

World Health Organization. (2022, January 10). Schizophrenia. Www.who.int. https://www.who.int/news-room/fact-sheets/detail/schizophrenia#:~:text=Some%20people%20with%20schizophrenia%20experience

www.ingramcontent.com/pod-product-compliance
Lightning Source LLC
Chambersburg PA
CBHW031515270326
41930CB00006B/409